Leveled Te

For Third Grade

Consultants

Kristin Kemp, M.A.Ed.
Reading Level Consultant
Fenton, Missouri

Wendy Conklin, M.A.
Gifted Education Consultant
Round Rock, Texas

Dennis Benjamin
Special Education Consultant
Prince William County Public Schools, Virginia

Marcela von Vacano
English Language Learner Consultant
Arlington County Schools, Virginia

Publishing Credits

Corinne Burton, M.A.Ed., *President*; Conni Medina, M.A.Ed., *Managing Editor*; Emily Rossman Smith, M.A.Ed., *Content Director*; Angela Johnson, M.F.A., M.S.Ed., *Editor*; Robin Erickson, *Multimedia Designer*; Kevin Pham, *Production Artist*; Danielle Deovlet, *Assistant Editor*

Image Credits

pp.54, 56, 58 World History Archive/Newscom; pp.113, 115, 117 David Starner/Wikimedia Commons; All other images from iStock, Shutterstock, or the public domain.

Standards

© 2004 Mid-continent Research for Education and Learning (McREL)
© 2006 Teachers of English to Speakers of Other Languages, Inc. (TESOL)
© Copyright 2010. National Governors Association Center for Best Practices and Council of Chief State School Officers. All rights reserved.

Shell Education

A division of Teacher Created Materials
5301 Oceanus Drive
Huntington Beach, CA 92649–1030
http://www.tcmpub.com/shell-education
ISBN 978–1–4258–1630–8
©2016 Shell Educational Publishing, Inc.

2

Table of Contents

How to Use This Product *(cont.)*

Tips for Managing the Product

How to Prepare the Texts

- When you copy these texts, be sure you set your copier to copy photographs. Run a few test pages and adjust the contrast as necessary. If you want the students to be able to appreciate the images, you will need to carefully prepare the texts for them.

- You also have full-color versions of the texts provided in PDF form on the Digital Resource CD. (See page 144 for more information.) Depending on how many copies you need to make, printing full-color versions and/or copying from a full-color version might work best for you.

- Keep in mind that you should copy two-sided to two-sided if you pull the pages out of the book. The shapes behind the page numbers will help you keep the pages organized as you prepare them.

Distributing the Texts

- Some teachers wonder about how to hand out the texts within one classroom. They worry that students will feel insulted if they do not get the same papers as their neighbors. The first step in dealing with these texts is to set up your classroom as a place where all students learn at their individual instructional levels. Making this clear as a fact of life in your classroom is key. Otherwise, the students may constantly ask about why their work is different. You do not need to get into the technicalities of the reading levels. Just state it as a fact that every student will not be working on the same assignment every day. If you do this, then passing out the varied levels is not a problem. Just pass them to the correct students as you circle the room.

- If you would rather not have students openly aware of the differences in the texts, you can try these strategies for passing out the materials.

  - Make a pile in your hands from the circle to triangle level. Put your fingers between the levels. As you approach each student, you pull from the correct section to meet his/her reading level. If you do not hesitate too much in front of each desk, the students will probably not notice.

  - Begin the class period with an opening activity. Put the texts in different places around the room. As students work quietly, circulate and direct students to the correct locations for retrieving the texts you want them to use.

  - Organize the texts in small piles by seating arrangement so that when you arrive at a group of desks you will have just the levels you need.

A Day in the Life of a Cowhand

A Cowhand's Morning

"Yee-haw!" yell the cowhands. They race off to round up the cattle. It's early in the morning. But their day is already beginning. There's so much to do!

Some cowhands work from sunup to sundown. Before the sun rises, the cowhands start their day. They put on the right clothes. They wear chaps, a bandana, and a hat. They also wear boots and spurs. Chaps and boots protect the cowhand's legs and ankles. They need protection since they ride through cactus and brush. Spurs look pointy, but they do not hurt a horse.

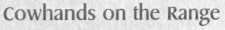

The cowhand gently taps the horse's ribs. The spurs on the boots tell the horse to go on. Bandanas and hats protect the cowhand's face and neck. There is wind, rain, and sun. A bandana can be used as a washcloth. The cowhand can clean things. The cloth can cover the eyes of a scared horse.

The cowhands get dressed for the day. They have a big breakfast. Then, they head out to work. They need plenty of energy to round up the cattle.

Cowhands on the Range

The cowhands head out to the range. They round up cattle. They take care of them. Animals might wander away from the ranch and cowhands have to find them. During the roundups, a team of cowhands spread out on the plains. They bring the cattle together. This is called a *cattle drive*.

While they herd cattle, cowhands rope the young calves. The calves need to be branded and get medical care. It may take three or four cowhands to work with one calf.

One cowhand ropes the calf by the horns. The other will rope him by the legs. The calf gets pulled to the ground. One or two cowhands brand the calf. They give it an ear tag and shots.

At midday, cowhands stop for lunch. A cook sets up the chuck wagon. He or she fixes the meal. The cook makes a quick lunch. The cowhands need to get back to herding the cattle. There's still a lot of work to do.

Cowhands spend the rest of the afternoon as they did the morning. They round up and care for the cattle. While they work, the cowhands are careful. They do not want to scare the cattle. If they get scared, they run and scatter. This is called a *stampede*. It can take hours to gather and calm them and get them back on the trail.

Before the cowhands settle in for the night, they care for their horses. The horses have worked hard all day, too. The cowhands remove their horses' saddles and feed them. Then, the horses are released on the open range so they can relax.

The cowhands start a campfire. They eat and tell stories. They might play cards or sing songs. Then, they go to sleep. They need to get up very early the next morning. It might be as early as three o'clock! Cowhands often rise before the sun.

Think About It!
What are cowhands, and what do they wear?

A Day in the Life of a Cowhand

A Cowhand's Morning

"Yee-haw!" yell the cowhands as they race off to round up the cattle. It's early in the morning, and their day is already beginning. There's so much to do!

Some cowhands work from sunup to sundown. Before the sun rises, the cowhands start their day by putting on the right clothes. These can include chaps, boots, spurs, a bandana, and a hat. Chaps and boots are used to protect the cowhand's legs and ankles. They need it since they ride through cactus and brush. Spurs may look dangerous, but they do not hurt a horse.

Instead, the cowhand gives the horse's ribs a gentle tap. The spurs attached to the boots urge the horse on. Bandanas and hats are used to protect the cowhand's face and neck from the wind, rain, and sun. A bandana can be used as a washcloth for the cowhand to clean things. It can also cover the eyes of a scared horse.

Once they are dressed for the day, the cowhands have a hearty breakfast before heading out. They need plenty of energy to round up the cattle.

Cowhands on the Range

After breakfast, the cowhands head out to the range. They round up and care for the cattle. They gather the animals that have wandered away from the ranch. During the roundups, a team of cowhands spreads out on the plains and brings the cattle together. This is called a *cattle drive*.

While they herd cattle, cowhands rope the young calves in order to brand them and give them medical care. It may take three or four cowhands to work with one calf.

As one cowhand ropes the calf by the horns, another will rope him by the legs, pulling him to the ground. One or two cowhands then brand, ear tag, and immunize the calf.

At midday, cowhands stop for lunch. A cook sets up the chuck wagon so he or she can fix the meal. The cook makes a quick lunch so the cowhands can get back to herding the cattle. There's still a lot of work to do.

Cowhands spend the rest of the afternoon as they did the morning. They round up and care for the cattle. While they work, the cowhands are careful not to startle the cattle. If cattle get scared, they run and scatter. This is called a *stampede*. It can take hours to gather and calm them and get them back on the trail.

Before the cowhands settle in for the night, they care for their horses. The horses have worked hard all day, too. The cowhands remove their horses' saddles and feed them. Then, they release the horses onto the open range to relax.

The cowhands prepare a campfire, eat, and tell stories. They play cards, sing songs, and get some sleep. They need to be ready to get up bright and early the next morning. Sometimes, it is as early as three o'clock! Cowhands often rise before the sun.

Think About It!
Why is it important for cowhands to wear specific clothing while working?

14

A Day in the Life of a Cowhand

A Cowhand's Morning

"Yee-haw!" yell the cowhands as they race off to round up the cattle. It's early in the morning, and their day is already beginning. There's so much to do!

Some cowhands work from sunup to sundown. Before the sun rises, the cowhands start their day by putting on the right clothes. These can include chaps, boots, spurs, a bandana, and a hat. Chaps and boots are used to protect the cowhand's legs and ankles while riding through cactus and brush. Spurs may look dangerous, but they are not meant to hurt a horse.

Instead, the horse is urged on by a gentle tap to its ribs from the spurs attached to the cowhand's boots. Bandanas and hats are used to protect the cowhand's face and neck from the wind, rain, and sun. A bandana can also be used as a washcloth for the cowhand to clean things or to cover the eyes of a scared horse.

Once they are dressed for the day, the cowhands have a hearty breakfast before heading out because they need all the energy they can get to round up the cattle.

Cowhands on the Range

After breakfast, the cowhands head out to the range to round up and care for the cattle. They gather the animals that have wandered away from the ranch. During the roundups, a team of cowhands fans out on the plains and brings the cattle together. This is called a *cattle drive*.

While they herd cattle, cowhands rope the young calves in order to brand them and give them medical care. It may take three or four cowhands to work with one calf.

15

As one cowhand ropes the calf by the horns, another will rope him by the legs, pulling him to the ground. One or two cowhands then brand, ear tag, and immunize the calf.

At midday, cowhands stop for lunch. A cook sets up the chuck wagon so he or she can fix the meal. The cook makes a quick lunch so the cowhands can get back to herding the cattle because there is still a lot of work to do.

Cowhands spend the afternoon in a similar way to their morning: they round up and care for the cattle. While they work, the cowhands are careful not to startle the cattle because if they get scared, they run and scatter. This is called a *stampede*, and it can take hours to gather and calm them and get them back on the trail.

Before the cowhands settle in for the night, they care for their horses. The horses have worked hard all day, too. The cowhands remove their horses' saddles, feed them, and release them onto the open range to relax.

The cowhands prepare a campfire, eat, and tell stories. They play cards, sing songs, and get some sleep. They need to be ready to get up bright and early the next morning, sometimes as early as three o'clock! Cowhands often rise before the sun.

Think About It!
Why are cowhands important on the range?

Sweet: Inside a Bakery

Sweet Treats

Chocolate chip, oatmeal raisin, sugar, and peanut butter are all types of cookies. All of these treats can be found in a bakery!

Most cookie batters start the same. They have flour, eggs, sugar, and butter. But bakers can add other treats. Candy, nuts, and raisins are just a few tasty extras. Cookies can be iced. Or they can be topped with sprinkles. Some bakeries sell a dozen kinds of cookies!

Cookie cutters come in lots of shapes, too. There are stars, hearts, and bells. There are even dog bones!

Cakes Are King!

Every party needs a cake. Many bakers make creative cakes. They design the cakes and make them fancy. These people are not only bakers. They are artists!

Some people want a special cake. It might show what they like to do. Cakes can have different shapes. They can be dogs or trains. They can look like drums. Or they can even be robots! Every cake is a work of art.

Cupcakes Are Big!

Cupcakes may be small, but they are a big business. Some places sell only cupcakes.

Years ago, most cupcakes were simple. They had chocolate or vanilla batter. They were frosted with simple icing.

Today, there are many kinds. There is red velvet and carrot cake. There are many more too. Food coloring can make icing any color. They can be filled with cream or fudge. The toppings have come a long way. Try sprinkles and nuts. Or fruit and candy bar crumbs!

(17)

Nuts for Doughnuts

Doughnuts are like simple round cakes. Sometimes, one can have a hole in the middle. They are big sellers! Each one starts as a thin piece of dough. They are in the shape of a ring. Each ring is placed in hot oil and fried. Some doughnuts are made of yeast. They can also be made with cake batter. Some have no hole in the middle. They might be filled with jam or cream. Not all doughnuts are round. They might be long bars. Others are twisted. They can be topped with glaze or sprinkles. Some have nuts or sugar. There are many yummy choices!

Muffin Madness

A muffin is like a cupcake and bread. It's not as sweet as a cupcake. It does not have icing. But it is not bread either. Muffins are made with a type of cake batter. The batter is poured. It goes into the cups of a muffin tin. The batter rises over the top as it cooks. This gives the muffin a giant mushroom shape. Extras such as fruit, poppy seeds, and chocolate chips can be baked inside.

Think About It!
What types of treats can be found in a bakery?

18

Sweet: Inside a Bakery

Sweet Treats

Chocolate chip, oatmeal raisin, sugar, and snicker doodle are all cookies. And they can all be found inside a bakery!

Most cookie batters start with flour, eggs, sugar, and butter. But bakers can add many other ingredients. Candy, nuts, vanilla, and raisins are just a few tasty extras. Cookies can be iced and topped with sprinkles. Some bakeries sell a dozen kinds of cookies!

Cookie cutters come in lots of shapes, too. There are stars, hearts, and snowflakes. There are even dog bones!

Cakes Are King!

No party is complete without a cake. Lots of bakeries make creative cakes. People who design and decorate these cakes are not only bakers. They are artists, too!

Some people like their cakes to say something about who they are or their hobbies. Some cakes take the shape of dogs, trains, houses, pianos, and even robots. Every cake is a delicious work of art!

Cupcakes Are Big!

Cupcakes may be small, but they are a big business. In fact, some bakeries sell *only* cupcakes.

Years ago, most cupcakes were simple. They were made with vanilla or chocolate cake batter. They were frosted with vanilla or chocolate icing.

Today, the batter might be red velvet or carrot cake. Food coloring can make the icing any color. Some cupcakes are filled with cream or fudge. And the toppings have come a long way. Try sprinkles and marshmallows or fruit and crumbled candy bars!

tNuts for Doughnuts

Doughnuts are like simple round cakes. They usually have a hole in the middle. The doughnut is one of the bakery's biggest sellers. Doughnuts are made with a skinny piece of dough in the shape of a ring. They are placed in hot oil and fried. There are yeast doughnuts and doughnuts made with cake batter. Some have no hole in the middle. They might be filled with jam or cream. Not all doughnuts are round. Some are long bars, others are twisted. They can be topped with glaze, sprinkles, chocolate, nuts, or sugar—or just about anything!

Muffin Madness

A muffin is a cross between a cupcake and bread. It's not as sweet as a cupcake and does not have frosting. But unlike bread, muffins are made with a type of cake batter. The batter is poured into the cups of a muffin tin. The batter rises over the top of the cup. This gives the finished muffin a giant mushroom shape. Extras such as fruit, poppy seeds, and chocolate chips can be baked inside.

Think About It!

What are some common ingredients used to make sweets in a bakery?

Sweet: Inside a Bakery

Sweet Treats

Chocolate chip, oatmeal raisin, sugar, snicker doodle. All of these delicious treats can be found inside a bakery!

Most cookie batters start with flour, eggs, sugar, and butter, but bakers can add many other ingredients. Candy, nuts, vanilla, and raisins are just a few tasty extras, or cookies can be iced and topped with sprinkles. Some bakeries sell a dozen kinds of cookies!

Cookie cutters come in lots of shapes, too. There are stars, hearts, and snowflakes—even dog bones!

Cakes Are King!

No party is complete without a cake. Lots of bakeries make creative cakes. People who design and decorate these cakes are not just bakers—they are artists, too!

Some people like their cakes to say something about who they are or their hobbies. Some cakes take the shape of animals, automobiles, trains, houses, instruments, and even robots. Every cake is a delicious work of art!

Cupcakes Are Big!

Cupcakes may be small, but they are a big business. In fact, some bakeries sell *only* cupcakes.

Years ago, most cupcakes were simple. They were made with vanilla or chocolate cake batter and were frosted with vanilla or chocolate icing.

Today, the batter might be red velvet or carrot cake. Food coloring can transform the icing into any color. Some bakers fill their cupcakes with buttercream or fudge. And the toppings have come a long way—try sprinkles and marshmallows or fruit and crumbled candy bars!

21

Nuts for Doughnuts

Doughnuts are like simple round cakes with a hole in the middle, but they are one of the bakery's biggest sellers. Doughnuts are made with a skinny piece of dough in the shape of a ring. Then, they are placed in hot oil and fried. There are yeast doughnuts and doughnuts made with cake batter. Some have no hole in the middle and are filled with jam or cream. Not all doughnuts are round. Some are long bars, and others are twisted. They can be topped with glaze, sprinkles, chocolate, nuts, or sugar—or just about anything!

Muffin Madness

A muffin is like a cross between a cupcake and bread. It's not as sweet as a cupcake and does not have frosting; but unlike bread, muffins are made with a type of cake batter. The batter is poured into the cups of a muffin tin. The batter rises over the top of the cup, which gives the finished muffin a giant mushroom shape. Extras such as fruit, poppy seeds, and chocolate chips can be baked inside.

Think About It!

If you could create your own bakery masterpiece, what ingredients would you use?

The Mystery of the Grand Bazaar

Zeyd Finds Bahir

The streets of the Grand Bazaar in Istanbul were busy. They were packed with colorful stalls. There were busy people. The air was filled with tasty smells from the food stands. The streets felt alive. The merchants were calling out to people. Among the action was a young man. His name was Zeyd. He was racing through the Bazaar. He ran fast through the crowds. He had a job to do.

Zeyd skipped between pots. He jumped over sleeping dogs. He ran through the furniture market. The whole time, he held tightly to a bundle. He stopped outside a rug stall. "Here you are, Akel," said Zeyd. He was out of breath. "This is a delivery from the food market."

Every day, Zeyd helped the traders of the Bazaar. He would run through all sixty-four streets. He went from one end to the other. He collected packages. He traded goods. In return, Zeyd was paid. He earned breakfast, lunch, and supper. Sometimes, he was given blankets or clothes. Once, a kind man gave him a rare jewel! Zeyd saw no point in gems. So he traded it for his favorite treat.

Zeyd and Akel shared a meal. They said goodbye. Zeyd began to walk to the Street of Jewels. These merchants often needed his help. They trusted Zeyd. Zeyd noticed something strange. A stack of rugs was moving. Zeyd looked closely. It was Bahir the monkey. He was digging around.

Bahir belonged to one of the jewelers. He was on the other side of the Bazaar.

"Are you lost, Bahir?" Zeyd bent down. Bahir leapt onto his shoulder. Together, they walked toward the Street of Jewels.

When they arrived a man wearing fancy clothes raced up to them. It was Jorim. He was a powerful jewelry trader.

"Bahir! There you are! You are a silly monkey!" Bahir leapt into Jorim's arms. "Thank you, young Zeyd."

Zeyd laughed. Jorim offered him a gold coin. But Zeyd shook his head. He told Jorim to think nothing of it. Coins meant nothing to him. Zeyd went home to his little room. It was above one of the market stands. It was cozy and the perfect size.

Silence in the Streets

In the morning, Zeyd woke. It was at his usual time. He waited a few moments. Something was different. It was silent. Zeyd wondered why he couldn't hear merchants talking. He couldn't hear children playing. He couldn't even hear donkeys braying.

Quickly, he ran downstairs. He entered the Bazaar. It was still. It was quiet. The stalls were closed. The streets were empty. He went to the Street of Food. Then, he could see a group. Zeyd pushed through the crowd. He wanted to see what was going on.

Who Is a Thief?

Jorim was standing at the front. "Who is the thief?" he yelled above the noise of the crowd. "Last night, someone stole from Akel. Until the thief confesses, the Bazaar will remain closed!" The merchants were angry. No one had ever stolen from the Bazaar before. Zeyd spotted Akel in the crowd and asked him what had been stolen. "A bag of gold coins," Akel said.

Zeyd nodded and walked through the angry crowd.

One by one, Jorim and Akel were questioning the merchants. Zeyd watched impatiently.

"YOUNG MAN!" Jorim's voice bellowed through the street. "Come!"

Startled, Zeyd entered the chamber.

"Sit!" ordered Jorim. Zeyd sat.

"Where were *you* last night, Zeyd?" Akel asked.

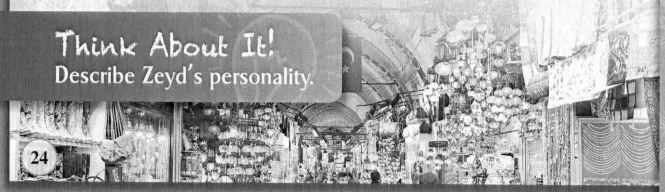

Think About It!
Describe Zeyd's personality.

The Mystery of the Grand Bazaar ⌃

Zeyd Finds Bahir

The streets of the Grand Bazaar in Istanbul were busy. They were packed with colorful stalls and busy people. The air was filled with delicious smells coming from the food stands. The streets were alive with the noise of merchants calling out to people.

Among the hustle and bustle, a young man named Zeyd was racing through the Bazaar. He darted nimbly through the crowds at the market. He had a job to do.

Zeyd skipped between pots and jumped over sleeping dogs. He ran through the furniture market. The whole time, he held tightly onto a delivery. He stopped outside a rug stall. "Here you are, Akel," said Zeyd, out of breath. "This is the delivery from the food market."

Every day, Zeyd helped the merchants of the Bazaar. He would run through all sixty-four streets. He went from one end to the other to collect packages or trade goods. In return, Zeyd would receive breakfast, lunch, and supper. Sometimes, he was even given blankets or clothing. Once, a kind merchant gave him a precious jewel! But Zeyd saw no point in trinkets. So he traded the jewel for his favorite pastry.

Zeyd and Akel shared a meal and said goodbye. Zeyd began to walk to the Street of Jewels. The jewel merchants often needed his help. They trusted Zeyd.

Suddenly, Zeyd noticed something strange. A stack of rugs was somehow moving. Zeyd looked more closely. It was Bahir the monkey, digging about.

Bahir belonged to one of the jewelers on the other side of the Bazaar.

"Are you lost, Bahir?" Zeyd bent down. Bahir leapt onto his shoulder. Together, they walked toward the Street of Jewels.

When they arrived, a man wearing fancy clothes raced up to them. It was Jorim, the powerful jewelry merchant.

"Bahir! There you are, you silly monkey!" Bahir leapt into Jorim's arms. "Thank you, young Zeyd."

 51630—Leveled Texts for Third Grade

Zeyd laughed. Jorim offered him a gold coin. But Zeyd shook his head. He told Jorim to think nothing of it. Coins meant nothing to him. Zeyd went home to his little room above one of the market stands. It was comfortable and the perfect size.

Silence in the Streets

In the morning, Zeyd woke at his usual time. But after a few moments, he realized something was different. It was silent. Zeyd wondered why he couldn't hear merchants chatting, children playing, or donkeys braying.

Quickly, he ran downstairs into the Bazaar. It was deserted. Everything was quiet. The stalls were closed and the streets were empty. It wasn't until he got to the Street of Food that he could see a throng. Zeyd pushed through the crowd to see what was going on.

Who Is a Thief?

Jorim was standing at the front. "Who among us is a thief?" he boomed above the hubbub of merchants. "Last night, someone stole from Akel, the rug merchant. Until the thief confesses, the Bazaar will remain closed!" The merchants surrounding him were angry. No one had ever stolen from the Bazaar before. Zeyd spotted Akel among the crowd and asked him what had been stolen. "A bag of gold coins," Akel replied.

Zeyd nodded and wandered through the angry crowd.

Zeyd saw that, one by one, the merchants were going into a chamber to be questioned by Jorim and Akel. Zeyd watched impatiently.

"YOUNG MAN!" Jorim's voice bellowed through the street. "Come!"

Startled, Zeyd entered the chamber.

"Sit!" ordered Jorim. Zeyd sat.

"Where were *you* last night, Zeyd?" Akel questioned.

Think About It!
Why doesn't Zeyd take trinkets or coins as payment for working?

The Mystery of the Grand Bazaar

Zeyd Finds Bahir

The streets of the Grand Bazaar in Istanbul were packed with colorful stalls and busy inhabitants. The air was filled with delicious aromas coming from the food and spice stands. The streets were alive with the noise of merchants calling out to passersby.

Among the hustle and bustle, a young man named Zeyd was racing through the Bazaar. He darted nimbly through the crowds at the market. He had a job to accomplish.

Zeyd skipped between pots, jumped over sleeping dogs, and sprinted through the furniture market. The whole time, he held tightly onto a delivery until he stopped outside a rug stall. "Here you are, Akel," whispered Zeyd breathlessly. "This is your delivery from the food market."

Every day, Zeyd helped the merchants of the Bazaar. He would dart from one end to the other, through all sixty-four streets, collecting packages or trading goods with merchants. In return, Zeyd would receive breakfast, lunch, and supper; sometimes, he was even given blankets or clothing. Once, a generous merchant gave him a precious jewel! But, since Zeyd saw no point in trinkets, he traded the jewel for his favorite pastry, baklava.

Zeyd and Akel shared a meal and said goodbye. Zeyd began to walk to the Street of Jewels because the jewel merchants trusted him and often needed his help.

Suddenly, he noticed something strange—a stack of rugs was moving mysteriously. Zeyd looked more closely and noticed Bahir the monkey, rummaging about.

Bahir belonged to one of the jewelers on the other side of the Bazaar.

"Are you lost, Bahir?" Zeyd bent down, and Bahir leapt onto his shoulder. Together, they walked toward the Street of Jewels.

When they arrived, a gentleman wearing expensive garments raced up to them. It was Jorim, the powerful jewelry merchant.

"Bahir! There you are, you silly monkey!" Bahir leapt into Jorim's arms. "Thank you, young Zeyd."

Zeyd laughed at the monkey. Jorim offered him a gold coin, but Zeyd shook his head and told Jorim to think nothing of it. Coins mean nothing, he thought, as he walked home to his little room located above one of the market stands. It was comfortable and the perfect size.

Silence in the Streets

In the morning, Zeyd woke at his usual time. But after a few moments, he realized something was different. It was silent. Zeyd wondered why he couldn't hear merchants chattering, children playing, or donkeys braying.

Quickly, he ran downstairs into the Bazaar, but it was deserted. Everything was quiet, the stalls were closed, and no one could be seen in the streets. It wasn't until he reached the Street of Food that he was able to see a throng of people. Zeyd pushed his way through the crowd to find out what was happening to cause such a commotion.

Who Is a Thief?

Jorim was standing at the front of the group of people. "Who among us is a thief?" he boomed above the hubbub of concerned merchants. "Last night, someone stole from Akel, the rug merchant. Until the thief confesses to the crime, the Bazaar will remain closed!" The merchants surrounding him were furious. No one had ever stolen anything from the Bazaar before. Zeyd spotted Akel standing among the crowd and asked him what had been stolen from his shop. "A bag of gold coins was taken," Akel replied.

Zeyd nodded and wandered through the angry crowd.

Zeyd saw that, one by one, the merchants were going into a chamber to be questioned by Jorim and Akel. Zeyd watched the process impatiently.

"YOUNG MAN!" Jorim's voice bellowed through the street. "Come!"

Startled, Zeyd entered the chamber.

"Sit!" ordered Jorim. Zeyd sat silently and waited.

"Where were *you* last night, Zeyd?" Akel questioned.

Think About It!
Based on the text, do you think Zeyd stole the bag of gold?

51630—Leveled Texts for Third Grade

How to Survive in the Jungle by the Person Who Knows

Disaster: I Love It!

Who am I? I'm Bradley D. Mented, that's who. I'm a wild and crazy star. I have a TV show. It's called *The Wild and Crazy Survivor Show!*

What a day I had today! Let me tell you about it. First, my plane ran out of fuel. Sure, I tried to glide. But then, the wings fell off, so I jumped out. Halfway down, I realized I didn't have my parachute. It was too late to go back for it. Luckily, I had a soft landing. I fell right into the mouth of a hungry hippo!

For a moment, I thought I might be in trouble. Its jaws were about to snap shut. But then, I remembered . . . hippos hate to be kissed. I kissed that hippo as hard as I could. It spat me out and made a face. Then, it sank under the water.

Now, here I am. I am lost and alone in the deep, dark jungle.

This is my kind of day!

By the way, I know I said I was alone. But I forgot about some people. The camera person, the director, and the animal catchers are here. And of course, there are medics and catering staff. There are also makeup artists and bodyguards. Apart from them, I am totally alone! Oh, and there are the 26 million TV viewers.

Beware What You Wear!

Wait until the next thrilling show. I will explain how you, too, can survive in the deep, dark jungle. If I can do it, so can you!

First, you'll need to decide what to wear. I suggest you buy a Swiss Army hat. If you push a button it can be used as a sleeping bag or a tent. Or, it can be a life jacket! Some people even use it as a hat.

Wear a very thick shirt. This is in case of tiger bites. Shoes are important, of course. It's best to buy the camouflage ones. That way, the snakes don't see you coming. Finally, only wear shorts that have been coated with anti-lion spray. The lions still might eat you, but they won't enjoy it!

Always Smile at a Crocodile

Here is the next thing you must know. You need to know how to survive an attack in a fierce jungle. There are two basic skills to learn.

A lot of people get scared if a crocodile is about to eat them. What a surprise! But crocs can smell fear. It makes them hungry. What you should do is smile. Don't run away. Just lie down. Close your eyes and smile. Three times out of ten, you won't be eaten! Or, try not moving. Stand still. Pretend you're invisible. This only works one in every ten times. But it makes a fantastic TV show!

Think About It!
Do you think this story is fiction or nonfiction? Explain your answer.

How to Survive in the Jungle by the Person Who Knows

Disaster: I Love It!

Who am I? I'm Bradley D. Mented, that's who. I'm a wild and crazy star with a TV show called *The Wild and Crazy Survivor Show!*

What a day I had today! Let me tell you about it. First, my plane ran out of fuel. Sure, I tried to glide, but then, the wings fell off. I jumped out, and halfway down, I realized I'd forgotten my parachute. It was too late to go back for it. Luckily, I had a soft landing. I fell right into the mouth of a hungry hippo!

For a moment, I thought I might be in trouble. But then, just as its jaws were about to snap shut, I remembered! Hippos hate to be kissed. I kissed that hippo as hard as I could. It spat me out, made a face, and sank under the water.

Now, here I am, lost and alone in the deepest, darkest jungle.

This is my kind of day!

By the way, when I said I was alone, I forgot to mention the camera operator, the director, and the animal wranglers. And of course, there are medics, catering staff, makeup artists, and bodyguards. Apart from them—and a TV audience of 26 million—I am totally alone!

Beware What You Wear!

In the next thrilling episode, I will explain how you, too, can survive in the deepest, darkest jungle. If I can do it, so can you!

The first thing you'll need to do is decide what to wear. I suggest you buy a Swiss Army hat, because with the simple push of a button, it can be used as a sleeping bag, a tent, or a life jacket. Some people even use it as a hat!

Wear a very thick shirt in case of tiger bites. Shoes are important, of course. It's best to buy the camouflage ones. That way, the snakes don't see you coming. Finally, only wear shorts that have been coated with anti-lion spray. The lions still might eat you, but they won't enjoy it!

Always Smile at a Crocodile

The next thing you must know is how to survive an attack in a fierce jungle. There are two basic skills to learn.

Surprisingly, a lot of people get scared if a crocodile is about to eat them. But crocs can smell fear. It makes them hungry. What you should do is smile. Don't run away. Just lie down, close your eyes, and smile. Three times out of ten, you won't be eaten! Or try standing perfectly still and pretending you're invisible. This only works one in every ten times, but it makes a fantastic TV show!

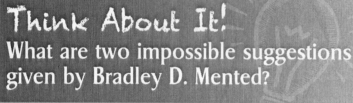

Think About It!
What are two impossible suggestions given by Bradley D. Mented?

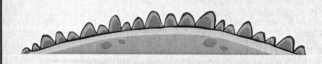

How to Survive in the Jungle by the Person Who Knows

Disaster: I Love It!

Who am I? Why, I'm Bradley D. Mented, that's who. I'm a wild and crazy celebrity, and I have an amazing TV show called *The Wild and Crazy Survivor Show!*

What a day I had today! Let me tell you about it. First, my plane ran out of gasoline. Sure, I tried to glide, but then the wings fell off. I jumped out, and halfway down I realized I'd forgotten my parachute. It was too late to go back for it, but luckily, I had a soft landing. I fell right into the mouth of a hungry hippopotamus!

For a moment, I thought I might be in trouble, but then, just as its jaws were about to snap shut, I remembered! Hippos hate to be kissed, so I kissed that hippo as hard as I could. It spat me out, made a face, and disappeared under the water.

Now, here I am, lost and alone in the deepest, darkest jungle.

This is my kind of day!

By the way, when I said I was alone, I forgot to mention just a few people, like the camera operator, the director, and the animal wranglers. And of course, there are physicians, catering staff, makeup artists, and bodyguards. Apart from them—and a TV audience of 26 million—I am totally and completely alone!

Beware What You Wear!

In the next thrilling episode, I will explain how you, too, can survive in the deepest, darkest jungle. If I can do it, so can you!

The first thing you'll need to do is make a decision about what to wear. I suggest you purchase a Swiss Army hat, because with the simple push of a button, it can be used as a sleeping bag, a tent, or a life jacket. Curiously enough, some people even use it as a hat!

Wear a very thick shirt in case of tiger bites. Shoes are important, of course, and I think it's best to buy the camouflage ones. That way, the snakes don't see you coming. Finally, only wear shorts that have been coated with anti-lion spray. The lions still might devour you, but they won't enjoy it!

Always Smile at a Crocodile

The next thing you must know is how to survive an attack in a ferocious jungle. There are two elementary skills to learn.

Surprisingly, a lot of people get frightened if a crocodile is about to eat them, but crocs can smell fear and it makes them ravenous. What you should do is smile—don't run away. Just lie down, close your eyes, and smile. Three times out of ten, you won't be eaten! Or you could try standing perfectly motionless and imagining you're invisible; this only works one in every ten times, but it makes a fantastic TV show!

Think About It!
What type of character is Bradley D. Mented? Can his advice be trusted?

Race to the Moon

Assembling the Ship

Mom pokes her head around the corner. "What are you guys up to?"

"We're going to build a rocket ship," I tell her.

"One that goes to the moon," adds Madison.

"Sounds fun," says Mom. "You can work on it in the basement. You'll find a lot of supplies for your rocket down there. Come on, I'll show you."

In the basement, Mom leads the way. We see two cardboard boxes in a corner. Beside them are things that are too big to fit in the boxes. They are covered in a sheet of black plastic.

"This is all the stuff that didn't sell when I held a yard sale," Mom explains. "You can use anything you want."

"Thank you!" we all cry.

Mom grabs a can of silver paint and some brushes from one of the boxes.

"You can use this, too. I've heard silver rockets are the fastest," she says.

Angelina frowns. "I thought red ones were the fastest."

"Oh, now I'm not sure." Mom digs deeper into the box. She finds a small can of red paint. "Here," she hands it to Timothy. "Splash some of this on, too. Just in case Angelina's right. Have fun!"

Mom walks out the door. Right away, we tip over the rest of the boxes. We want to see what treasures we can find.

There are a lot of clothes, books, magazines, and old CDs and DVDs. We also see some balls of yarn, a broken toaster, and a dartboard. And there are still a lot more bits and pieces.

"This is just junk. There's nothing here to help us build a rocket," declares Timothy.

"What about these?" Madison holds up two beach umbrellas.

"They can be the roof of the rocket!" says Angelina.

"They'll keep off the rain, too," I add.

Timothy opens and closes the umbrellas to make sure they're working. "Yeah," he says. "You're right. These will work, and we can use the boxes for the sides of the ship."

Madison lifts up the plastic sheet and turns to us, smiling. "Check this out!"

We're looking at an exercise bike. It's old and the seat is cracked. But it still works. I give the wheels a spin.

Timothy smiles at her. "Madison," he says, "you've found our engine!"

Think About It!
What are the kids using to make their rocket?

Race to the Moon

Assembling the Ship

Mom pokes her head around the corner and asks, "What are you guys up to?"

"We're going to build a rocket ship," I answer her.

"One that goes to the moon," adds Madison.

"Sounds marvelous," says Mom. "You can work on it in the basement. You'll find a lot of materials for your rocket down there. Come on, I'll show you."

In the basement, Mom leads the way to two cardboard boxes in a corner. Beside them, covered by a sheet of black plastic, are things that are too big to fit in the boxes.

"These are all the items that didn't sell when I hosted a garage sale," Mom explains. "You can use anything you want."

"Thank you!" we all cry in unison.

Mom grabs a can of silver paint and some brushes from one of the boxes.

"You can use this, too, because I've heard silver rockets are the fastest," she says.

Angelina frowns and says, "I thought red ones were the fastest."

"Oh, now I'm not sure," Mom says, digging deeper into the box and finding a small can of red paint. "Here," she hands it to Timothy. "Splash some of this on, too, just in case Angelina's right. Have fun!"

The moment Mom walks out the door, we tip over the rest of the boxes to see what treasures we can find.

There are a lot of books, clothing, magazines, old CDs and DVDs, some balls of yarn, a broken toaster, a dartboard, and a lot more bits and pieces.

"This is just junk. There's nothing here to help us build a rocket," declares Timothy.

"What about these?" Madison holds up two beach umbrellas.

"They can be the roof of the rocket!" says Angelina.

"They'll keep off the rain, too," I add.

Timothy opens and closes the umbrellas to make sure they're working. "Yeah," he says. "You're right. These will work, and we can use the boxes for the sides of the ship."

Madison lifts up the plastic sheet and turns to us, smiling. "Check this out!"

We're looking at an exercise bike. It's old and the seat is cracked, but I can tell it still works as I give the wheels a spin.

Timothy congratulates her and says, "Madison, you've found our engine!"

Think About It!
Describe Madison's, Angelina's, and Timothy's personalities.

Race to the Moon

Assembling the Rocket

Mother pokes her head around the corner and inquires, "What's happening with you guys?"

"We're planning to construct a rocket ship," I answer.

"One that travels to the moon," adds Madison.

"Sounds marvelous," says Mother. "You can work in the basement; you'll find several materials for your spacecraft down there. Come on, I'll show you."

In the basement, Mother leads the way to two cardboard boxes in a corner. Beside them, covered by a sheet of black plastic, are the enormous shapes of mystery possessions too large to fit in the boxes.

"These are the items nobody purchased when I hosted a garage sale," Mother explains. "You are welcome to anything that might be helpful."

"Thank you!" we all exclaim in unison.

Mother finds a canister of silver paint and some paintbrushes in one of the boxes.

"You can use this, too, because I've heard silver rockets are the fastest," she says.

Angelina frowns, disappointed, and says, "I always thought red ones were the fastest."

"Oh, now I'm not sure," Mother says, digging deeper into the box and finding a small container of red paint. "Here," she says, handing it to Timothy, "splash some of this on, too, just in case Angelina's right. Have fun!"

The moment Mother walks out the door, we spill the rest of the boxes to see what treasures and resources we can find.

There are several books and stacks of clothing, magazines, old CDs and DVDs, some balls of yarn, a broken toaster, a dartboard, and a lot more bits and pieces.

"This is just garbage. There's nothing here to assist us in building our rocket," declares Timothy.

"What about these?" Madison holds up two beach umbrellas.

"They can be the roof of the rocket!" says Angelina.

"They'll keep off the rain, too," I add.

Timothy opens and closes the umbrellas to ensure that they're working. "Yeah," he says, "you're right. These will work, and we can use the boxes for the sides of the ship."

Madison lifts up the plastic sheet and turns to us, smiling. "Check this out!"

We're looking at an exercise bike. It's old and the seat is cracked, but I can tell it still works as I give the wheels a spin.

Timothy congratulates her and says, "Madison, you've found our engine!"

Think About It!
If the bike doesn't work as an engine, how might the kids' personalities help them problem solve?

Our Vacation Budget

To the Beach

Mom and Dad have fun news. We are going to the beach. Our trip will be in eight weeks. There is so much to do. My sister Keandra and I can't wait!

Mom has made a budget. This is a plan. It will help Mom and Dad plan how much the trip will cost. It will help them a second way. They can find out how much to save. What they save will pay for our trip.

Eight Weeks to Go

Mom showed me a list. It says how much she thinks things will cost. These are our expenses. They are things such as money for gas and food. The beach house costs money, too. Mom also plans for fun stuff called entertainment.

She even planned for extra costs. Mom says it's for "just in case!"

Mom is giving me $25.00. Keandra gets $25.00, too! We can spend it at the beach. Mom says the whole trip will cost $1,500.00.

Will We Have Enough Money?

Costs are only part of Mom's budget. Saving money is also a part. Mom and Dad have been saving. They have $1,100.00.

Mom and Dad have a plan. They will save $50.00 per week starting now! The vacation is only eight weeks away.

What About Keandra and Me?

I will get $25.00 from mom. But I think I will need more. I want to do many things at the beach. Keandra thinks she will need more, too.

Mom told us to make a list. It has our trip costs. This will help us. We need to work out how much money we will need. We know we'll need more money!

My sister and I will have to make a budget. We can make a plan. It will show how much money we should save. First, we work out our income. I get a

$5.50 per week allowance. I will save it all for the next eight weeks. Then, I will add $25.00. This is my money from Mom. How much will I have?

Keandra has more money than I do! She and I get the same allowance. Plus, she earns $15.75 per week babysitting. *And* she had saved $20.40.

Four Weeks to Go

We have all been saving for our trip. But we had some bad luck. Our refrigerator broke! Fixing it costs $400.00. This unexpected expense will come out of the beach trip savings. Ouch!

Think About It!
According to the passage, what are *unexpected expenses*?

42

Our Vacation Budget

To the Beach

Mom and Dad said we are going to the beach. Our vacation will be in eight weeks. There will be so much to do. My sister Keandra and I can't wait!

Mom has made a vacation budget. The budget is a plan. It will help Mom and Dad figure out how much the vacation will cost. It will also help them figure out how much money to save to pay for it.

Eight Weeks to Go

Mom showed me how much she thinks things will cost. These are called our expenses. They include money for gas and food. The beach house costs money, too. Mom also plans for fun stuff. She calls it entertainment.

The budget even has money for unexpected expenses. Mom says it's for "just in case!"

Mom is giving me $25.00! Keandra gets $25.00, too! She says we can spend it at the beach. Mom says the whole trip will cost $1,500.00.

Will We Have Enough Money?

Expenses are only part of Mom's budget. Saving money is also part of the budget. Mom and Dad have already saved $1,100.00.

Mom and Dad plan to save $50.00 per week between now and the vacation. The vacation is only eight weeks away.

What About Keandra and Me?

I will need more than $25.00 to pay for the things I want to do at the beach. Keandra thinks she will need more, too.

Mom told us to make a list of our vacation expenses. This will help us work out how much money we will need. We know we'll need more money!

Keandra and I will have to make a budget. That way, we can plan how much money we will be able to save. First, we work out our income. I get a $5.50 per week allowance. I will save it all for the next eight weeks. Then, I will add it to the $25.00 vacation spending money. How much will I have?

Keandra has more money than I do! She gets the same allowance as I do. She also earns $15.75 per week babysitting. *And* she's already got $20.40 in savings.

Four Weeks to Go

We have all been saving for our vacation. But yesterday we had some bad luck. Our refrigerator broke! It was fixed, but it cost $400.00. This will come out of the vacation savings. Ouch!

Think About It!
Why is making a budget a good idea for the family in the story?

44

Our Vacation Budget

To the Beach

Mom and Dad said we are going to the beach in eight weeks for a vacation. There will be so much to do. My sister Keandra and I can't wait!

Mom has made a vacation *budget*, which is a plan that will help Mom and Dad figure out how much the vacation will cost. It will also help them figure out how much money to save to pay for it.

Eight Weeks to Go

Mom showed me how much she thinks things will cost; these are called our expenses. They include money for gas and food and, of course, the beach house costs money, too. Mom also plans for fun stuff, which she calls entertainment.

The budget even has money for unexpected expenses. Mom says it's for "just in case!"

Mom is giving Keandra and me $25.00 each for us to spend on the vacation. Mom says the whole vacation will cost $1,500.00.

Will We Have Enough Money?

Expenses are only part of Mom's budget. Saving money is also part of the budget, and Mom and Dad have already saved $1,100.00.

Mom and Dad plan to save $50.00 per week between now and the vacation. The vacation is only eight weeks away.

What About Keandra and Me?

I will need more than $25.00 to pay for the things I want to do at the beach. Keandra thinks she will need more, too.

Mom told us to make a list of our vacation expenses because this will help us figure out how much money we will need. We'll definitely need more money!

45

Keandra and I will have to make a budget. That way, we can plan how much money we will be able to save. First, we work out our income. I get $5.50 per week allowance. If I save it all for the next eight weeks and then add it to the $25.00 vacation spending money, how much will I have?

Keandra has a lot more money than I do! She gets a $5.50 allowance, like I do, but she also earns $15.75 per week babysitting. *And* she's already got $20.40 in savings.

Four Weeks to Go

We have all been saving for our vacation, but yesterday our refrigerator broke! It was fixed, but it cost $400.00, and this will come out of the vacation savings. Ouch!

Think About It!

What are some ways the family could save extra money after the repair?

Measuring Time

Time in Races

It is fun to watch a race. But it can also be a big deal. If some athletes win races they can earn money. They might break a world record. If this happens, they can earn even more money!

Long ago, people timed races. They held a stopwatch. It was manual. But it could not show small times. It could only show up to 0.5 of a second. Today, new timers are used. They are digital. A race can be timed to 0.01 of a second.

Times on the Track

A new watch was made. It did not need to be held. It was automatic. It was first used in 1932. This was during the Olympics. But the watch could not show small times. It could only show up to 0.1 of a second.

In 1932, there was a race. It was 100 meters long. One man won the race. He took 10.3 seconds. One man won third place. He took 10.4 seconds. Their times were very close. They were only one tenth of a second apart! This is 0.1 seconds. It was a fast race. So this seemed like a long time.

GO!

Things have changed now. There is a start gun. It starts a digital timer. These show small times. They show down to 0.01 of a second!

The starting blocks have speakers. Runners hear the start gun. Sound goes through the speakers. They all hear it at the same time.

Take-Off Time

Runners hear the sound of the gun. They take off. A runner might go too soon. This is called a *false start*. All of the runners get a warning. If it happens again, then the runner has to leave. This is to be *disqualified*.

A new finish line was made. It was at the 2004 Olympics. It had a laser beam across it. Runners crossed the finish line. This "broke" the beam and stopped the timer.

Times in the Pool

People swam in the past. They would race. They were timed with a stopwatch. People stood by the pool. They timed the race. A swimmer would touch the wall. Then, the time stopped.

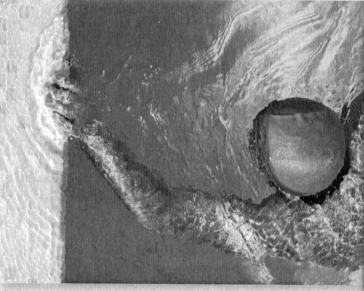

Today, touch pads are used. They time races. Swimmers touch them at the end of a race.

Starting blocks have sensors. They know if a swimmer makes a false start. There are also cameras. They are under the water. They make sure swimmers obey the rules.

Touch pads were first used in 1968 at the Olympics. Touch pads measure time. They are accurate. Touch pads show down to 0.001 of a second.

Think About It!
What are some ways races are timed?

Measuring Time

Time in Races

It has always been important to know who won a race. But these days, it is even more important. Athletes can earn money if they win races. They might break a world record. Then, they can earn even more!

Long ago, people used manual stopwatches. They timed races. But they could only measure down to 0.5 of a second. Today, digital timers are used. Races are timed down to 0.01 of a second.

Times on the Track

Automatic stopwatches were invented. They were first used at the 1932 Olympics. But they could only measure down to 0.1 of a second.

In 1932, a man won the 100-meter race. He finished in 10.3 seconds. A different man won third place. He finished the race in 10.4 seconds. Their times were only one tenth of a second apart. This is a long time in such a fast race!

GO!

These days, the starter gun starts a digital timer. These timers can measure smaller times. They can go down to 0.01 of a second!

The starting blocks have speakers. Runners hear the starter gun through the speakers. They all hear it at the same time.

Take-Off Time

Runners hear the sound of the gun, then they take off. A runner might take off too early. This is called a *false start*. All runners are given a warning after a false start. Then, the next runner who makes a false start has to leave. He or she is *disqualified*.

The finish line at the 2004 Olympics was new. It had a laser beam across it. Runners "broke" the beam when they crossed the line. This stopped the timer.

Times in the Pool

In the past, stopwatches were used to time swimming races. People stood at the end of the pool. They kept the time of the race. The time was stopped when a swimmer touched the wall.

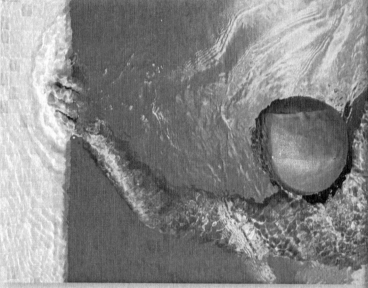

Today, touch pads are used to time races. Swimmers touch them at the end of a race.

Starting blocks have sensors in them. They can tell if a swimmer makes a false start. There are even cameras under the water. They check that swimmers obey the rules.

Touch pads were first used at the 1968 Olympics. They can measure time accurately. Touch pads measure time down to 0.001 of a second.

Think About It!
How are running and swimming races timed differently?

Measuring Time

Time in Races

It has always been important to know who won a race, but these days, it is even more important. Athletes can earn money if they win races. They can earn even more if they break a world record!

Long ago, manual stopwatches were used to time races, but they could only measure down to 0.5 of a second. Today, digital timers are used to time races. Races are timed down to 0.01 of a second.

Times on the Track

Automatic stopwatches were used for the first time at the 1932 Olympics. But they could only measure down to 0.1 of a second.

In 1932, the winner of the men's 100-meter race finished the race in 10.3 seconds. The athlete who finished third crossed the finish line in 10.4 seconds. One tenth of a second is a long time in such a fast race!

GO!

These days, the starter gun starts a digital timer. Today's timers are able to measure down to 0.01 of a second!

The starting blocks have speakers. Runners hear the starter gun through the speakers, and they all hear it at the same time.

Take-Off Time

Runners take off when they hear the sound of the gun. If a runner takes off before that, it is a *false start*. All runners are given a warning after a false start. Then, the next runner who makes a false start is *disqualified* from the race.

The finish line at the 2004 Olympics had a laser beam across it. Runners "broke" the beam when they crossed the line. This stopped the timer.

Times in the Pool

In the past, stopwatches were used to time swimming races. Timekeepers stood at the end of the pool. The time was stopped when a swimmer touched the wall.

Today, touch pads are used to time races. Swimmers touch them at the end of a race.

Starting blocks have sensors in them. They can tell if a swimmer makes a false start. Underwater cameras check that swimmers obey the swimming rules.

Touch pads were first used at the 1968 Olympics. Touch pads can measure time accurately, down to 0.001 of a second.

Think About It!

In what ways are digital timers better than manual stopwatches?

Natural Measures

Measure Length

Long ago, people did not measure as we do now. They used their body parts to find length. People used their hands and arms. Hands could measure clothes. They could also use their hands or feet. People used their body to measure buildings.

In ancient Egypt, they measured length. They used the cubit. It was the length of part of a man's arm. It went from his elbow to the tip of his middle finger. This was used to measure land. The Nile River would flood. A cubit could find how much it flooded.

Measure Volume

People used seeds to measure. They would measure volume. The seeds were poured in a bowl. It would fill up. Then, the seeds were counted.

People need to know the volume of the bowl. What if you wanted to buy some rice? You would want to know how big the bowl was. Once you figured out the volume, then you would pay!

Measure Weight

People used seeds and stones to measure how heavy things were. The price of some goods was based on weight.

Carob seeds were used. They weighed gold. They weighed diamonds, too! The weight of the seed was called a *carat*. Today some items are still weighed in carats. A carat weighs 0.2 of a gram.

Measure Time

People use the sun to help tell time. If the sun is high in the sky this means it is noon. A sundial was a good way to tell time. The sun's light hits the pointer on the dial. This makes a shadow. The shadow points to a number. This number shows the time.

Making Measurements the Same

Things in nature were used to measure. It was easy. But hands and seeds caused a problem. They were not all the same size. So, length or weight was not always the same.

People in Egypt made a cubit stick. It was standard. Its length was 20.6 inches (52.4 centimeters). Any person could use these sticks. The cubits would be the same length.

People from other places started to trade. They agreed on how things would be measured. This meant they would be the same.

In 1875, many countries agreed to change to standard measurements. Their goal was to make all of them the same. So now, a meter in France is the same as a meter in the United States. But the units are still not the same all over the world. People in the United States show distance in miles. But others use kilometers.

Think About It!

What are some ways that things are measured?

Natural Measures

Measuring Length

Long ago, people did not have measuring sticks. Instead, body parts were used to find length. People used their hands and arms. Hands were used to measure clothes. They also used their hands or feet. People also used their body parts to measure buildings.

In ancient Egypt, length was measured with the cubit. A cubit was the length of part of a man's arm. It was from his elbow to the tip of his middle finger. A cubit was used to measure areas of land. It was also used to measure the level of flooding of the Nile River.

Measuring Volume

People used seeds to measure the volume of a bowl. The seeds were poured into the bowl until it was full. Then, the seeds were counted.

It is important to know the volume of a bowl. Imagine you wanted to buy some rice. You would want to know how big the bowl was before you paid!

Measuring Weight

People used seeds and stones to measure how heavy things were. The price of many goods was based on the weight.

Carob seeds were used for weighing gold and diamonds. The weight of a carob seed was called a *carat*. Gold and diamonds are still measured in carats. Today, a carat weighs 0.2 of a gram.

Measuring Time

People use the sun to help tell time. When the sun is high in the sky, it is noon. A sundial was a better way to tell time. The sun's light hits the pointer on a sundial and makes a shadow. The shadow points to a number. This number shows the time.

Making Measurements the Same

It was easy to use natural things to measure. But bodies, seeds, and stones were not all the same size. So measurements were not always the same.

The Egyptians made a standard cubit stick. The standard cubit stick was 20.6 inches (52.4 centimeters). Everyone could measure cubits of the same length with these sticks.

People from other places started to trade with each other. They agreed on how things would be measured. This meant their measurements would be the same.

In 1875, many countries agreed to make all measurements the same. So now, a meter in France is the same length as a meter in the United States. But units of measurement still are not the same in all countries. People in the United States measure distance in miles. But Australians use kilometers.

Think About It!

What are some problems with the idea of measuring length using body parts?

Natural Measures

Measuring Length

Long ago, people did not have measuring sticks. Instead, body parts were used for measuring length. These included hands and arms. Hands were used to measure clothes. They had to use their hands or their feet. People also used their body parts to measure buildings.

In ancient Egypt, a measurement of length was the cubit. A cubit was the length of part of a man's arm from his elbow to the tip of his middle finger. A cubit was used to measure areas of land. It was also used to measure the level of flooding of the Nile River.

Measuring Volume

People used seeds to measure the volume of a container. The seeds were poured into the container until it was full, and then the seeds were counted.

It is important to know the volume of a container. Imagine you wanted to buy a container of rice. You would want to know how big the container was before you paid!

Measuring Weight

People used seeds and stones to measure how heavy things were because the price of many goods was based on their weight.

Carob seeds were used for weighing gold and diamonds. The weight of a carob seed was called a *carat*. Gold and diamonds are still measured in carats. Today, a carat weighs 0.2 of a gram.

Measuring Time

People use the position of the sun to help tell time. When the sun is high in the sky, it is noon. A sundial was a better way to tell time. When the sun's light hits the pointer on a sundial, it makes a shadow. The shadow points to a number, and this number shows the time.

Making Measurements the Same

It was easy to use natural things to measure, but bodies, seeds, and stones were not all the same size. So measurements were not always the same.

The Egyptians made a standard cubit stick, which measured 20.6 inches (52.4 centimeters). Everybody could measure cubits of the same length with these sticks.

People from different places started to trade with each other. They agreed on how things would be measured. This meant their measurements would be the same.

In 1875, many countries agreed to make all measurements the same. So now, a meter in France is exactly the same length as a meter in the United States, for example. But units of measurement still are not the same in all countries. People in the United States measure distances in miles; however, Australians use kilometers.

Think About It!

How do standard units of measurement help make things fair?

My Lemonade Stand

How It Started

I wanted to buy a bike. It was summer break. But I had no money. Dad said he had a lemonade stand when he was a kid. What a fun idea!

Day 1: My First Sale

Dad took me to the store. He helped me shop. He even lent me money. I paid for the supplies. It cost $54.00. I will pay dad back. But first, I have to sell lemonade. I made some and set up the stand. I charged $1.00 per cup. Mr. Ling came first. He liked it a lot. He bought a second cup!

Today was great! I sold 70 cups. I got $70.00! Dad says that is my *income*. Now, I need to subtract my costs. I spent $54.00 at the store. What is left over is my *profit*. I can save that for my bike!

Day 2: Ice

I will add ice. This will help the drinks stay cool. It will also take less to fill each cup. I will add ice to Mom's recipe. Now, I will get 18 cups per batch. I used to get only 12. So I will earn more money!

The ice worked. I had 50 cups of drinks. They were left over from the day before. I added ice. That stretched it to 75 cups. I sold out! I made $75.00. Dad went to the store. He bought more cups. I had to spend some money. I had to pay for the cups. But I still made a profit.

Day 3: Jill Murray

I bought more stuff and made more lemonade. But Jill Murray is a girl from school. She has her own lemonade stand now. She will hurt my business! I made flyers. My brother, Mike, handed out flyers to people.

Jill ruined my sales. I only sold 30 cups today. That is less than half of what I sold the day before. But I spent more money, and I made more lemonade. I spent $66.00 at the store. I also gave Mike $5.00 because he helped with the flyers. Plus, all my ice melted. I can't stretch the drinks out again. What am I going to do?

Day 4: My Secret Weapon!

I had a great idea! I looked on the Internet. I found out how to make blue lemonade. I spent $5.00 on frozen blueberries. I added it to my first recipe. And this was the result: a sell-out! I had 120 cups left over from the day before. The berries stretched that to 135 cups. But I spent $5.00 on the berries. I earned $135.00, and I spent $5.00. That equals a $130.00 profit!

Think About It!
What happens on the third day?

My Lemonade Stand

How It Started

I wanted to buy a bike during summer break. But I had no money. Dad said he had a lemonade stand when he was a kid. It sounded like a fun idea!

Day 1: My First Sale

Dad helped with the shopping. He even lent me the money to pay for everything. It cost $54.00. I will pay him back when I sell some lemonade. I made some lemonade and set up the stand. I charged $1.00 for a cup of lemonade. Mr. Ling was my first customer. He liked the lemonade so much that he bought a second cup!

Today was great! I sold 70 cups and got $70.00! Dad says that is called my *income*. Now, I need to subtract my costs. I spent $54.00 at the store. What is left over is my *profit*. That can go toward my bike!

Day 2: Ice

If I use ice, the drinks will stay cooler. Also, it takes less lemonade to fill each cup. I will add some ice to Mom's recipe. This means I get 18 cups instead of 12 per batch. So I will earn more money!

The ice worked. I had 50 cups of lemonade left over from yesterday. With ice, I stretched them to 75 cups. And I sold out. That is $75.00 dollars! Dad went to the store for more cups. I had to spend money to pay for the cups. But I still made a profit.

61

Day 3: Jill Murray

I bought more stuff and made more lemonade. But now Jill Murray from school has her own lemonade stand. She will ruin my business! I made some flyers. I asked Mike, my brother, to hand them out to people.

Jill Murray ruined my sales. I only sold 30 cups. That is less than half of what I sold yesterday. But I have spent more money making more lemonade! I spent $66.00 on supplies. I also gave Mike $5.00 for helping with the flyers. Plus, all my ice melted. I won't be able to stretch the lemonade out again. What am I going to do?

Day 4: My Secret Weapon!

I had a great idea! I found a recipe on the Internet for blue lemonade. I added $5.00 worth of frozen blueberries to my original recipe. And this was the result: a sell-out! I had 120 cups left over from yesterday. The blueberries stretched that to 135 cups. But I spent $5.00 on blueberries. $135.00 earned – $5.00 spent = $130.00 profit!

Think About It!
How does the third day change how he sells lemonade?

My Lemonade Stand

How It Started

I wanted to buy a bicycle during summer vacation, but I had no money. Dad said he had a lemonade stand when he was a kid. It sounded like an exciting idea!

Day 1: My First Sale

Dad assisted with the shopping and even let me borrow the money to pay for everything. It cost $54.00, but I will pay him back when I sell some lemonade. I made some lemonade and set up the stand. I charged $1.00 for a cup of lemonade. Mr. Ling was my first customer, and he liked the lemonade so much that he bought a second cup!

Today was amazing! I sold 70 cups and got $70.00! Dad explained that the money I made is called my *income*, but now I need to subtract my costs. I spent $54.00 at the store. What is left over is my *profit*; that money can go toward my bike!

Day 2: Ice

If I use ice, the drinks will stay cooler and it will take less lemonade to fill each cup. I will add some ice to Mom's recipe. This means I get 18 cups instead of 12 per batch, so I will earn more money!

The ice worked! I had 50 cups of lemonade left over from yesterday. By adding ice, I stretched them to 75 cups, and I sold out! That is $75.00! Dad went shopping at the store for more cups. I had to spend money to pay for the cups, but I still made a profit.

Day 3: Jill Murray

I bought more ingredients and made more lemonade. But now Jill Murray from school has started her own lemonade stand. She will destroy my business! I made some flyers and asked Mike, my brother, to hand them out to people.

Jill Murray ruined my sales. I only sold 30 cups, which is less than half of what I sold yesterday. But I have spent more money making more lemonade! I spent $66.00 on supplies, and I gave Mike $5.00 for helping with the flyers. Plus, all my ice melted, and I won't be able to stretch the lemonade out again. What am I going to do?

Day 4: My Secret Weapon!

I had a brilliant idea! I found a recipe on the Internet for blue lemonade, so I added $5.00 worth of frozen blueberries to my original recipe. And this was the result: a sell-out! I had 120 cups left over from yesterday. The blueberries stretched that to 135 cups, but I spent $5.00 on the blueberries. $135.00 earned – $5.00 spent = $130.00 profit!

Think About It!
If his business encounters another obstacle, like he did on day 3, what do you think he might do?

The World of Trade

What Is Trade?

The word *trade* means to buy, sell, or swap goods or services. A *good* is a thing you can own. Maybe you own a skateboard. A *service* is a thing someone does for you. Some people have newspapers delivered every day. That is a service.

Bartering

People first traded by bartering. Bartering is where goods and services are swapped with each other. No money is used. I have corn, but I want beads. You have beads, but you want corn. We could swap corn for beads. People have bartered for thousands of years. They still do it today.

Bartering takes a lot of work. First, you have to bargain. You have to agree on many ideas. How much are things worth? How much corn should I trade for beads? What if I want your beads, but you do not want my corn? We would have to find someone else who wants corn. She would need to have something that you want, such as milk. Then, I could give her my corn. She could give you her milk. You could give me your beads. It is all very tricky!

Money

People had to agree on what items to trade when they would barter. They traded things that they all found useful. Many things were used as money.

Over time, coins were made from metal. Metal coins worked well as money. People agreed that metal was worth a lot. Metal coins are easy to carry. They do not wear out or fall apart.

Money made trading easier. You do not want my corn. So I sell it to someone who does. I take money for it. Then, I give you money for your beads. You can spend that money on something you need.

Bills make it easy to carry money. A single bill is worth many coins. It would be hard to carry a bag of coins all the time. Coins can get really heavy! Coins let us buy things for less than $1.00. The U.S. dollar is split into 100 cents. If something costs 25 cents, you can pay with a dollar. You get 75 cents back.

Markets

Markets are places where people go to trade. People have been going to markets for thousands of years. The first markets were held outside. The *agora* was a market in ancient Greece. Markets are a good way to trade. People can look around. They can see what is for sale. Then, they can try to get the best deal for what they want.

Auction websites are also markets. You can look at what is for sale. You can still try to get the best deal. But you do not have to walk around. You can do your shopping on a computer.

Think About It!
What is bartering?

The World of Trade

What Is Trade?

The word *trade* means to purchase, sell, or swap goods or services. *Goods* are things you can own, like a skateboard. *Services* are things people do for you. For example, some families have newspapers delivered daily. That is a service.

Bartering

People first traded by bartering. Bartering is where goods and services are swapped with each other. No money is used in bartering. I have corn but want beads; you have beads but want corn. We could barter corn for beads. People have been bartering for thousands of years, and they continue to do it today.

Bartering is time-consuming work. First, you have to bargain and agree what things are worth. How much corn should I trade for beads? Second, what if I want your beads, but you don't want my corn? We'd have to find someone else who wants corn. She would need to have something you wanted—like milk. Then, I could give her my corn, she could give you her milk, and you could give me your beads. It's all very complicated!

Money

People had to agree on what items to trade when bartering. They traded items they all found useful. Many things were used as money.

Over time, people made coins from metals. Metal coins worked well as money because everyone agreed that metal was valuable. Metal coins are easy to carry, and they do not wear out or fall apart.

Money made trading easier. You don't want my corn, so I sell it to someone who does. I take money for it and give you the money for your beads. You can spend that money on anything you need.

Bills make it easier to carry money because a single bill is worth many coins. It would be hard to carry a heavy bag filled with coins all the time! Coins let us buy things for less than $1.00. The U.S. dollar is divided into 100 cents, so if something costs 25 cents, we can pay with a dollar and get 75 cents back.

Markets

Markets are places where people go to trade. People have been going to markets for thousands of years. The first markets were held outside. The *agora* was a market in ancient Greece. Markets are a good way to trade. People can look around, find out what is for sale, and then try to get the best deal for what they want.

Internet auction sites are also markets. You can research what is for sale. You can still try to get the best deal. But you do not have to walk around. You can do your shopping on a computer.

Think About It!
Why is using money a simpler system of trading than bartering?

68

The World of Trade

What Is Trade?

The definition of *trade* is to purchase, sell, or swap goods or services. *Goods* are items you can possess, such as a skateboard. *Services* are things people do for you; for example, some families have newspapers delivered daily. That is a service.

Bartering

People first traded by bartering, which is swapping goods and services with each other. Bartering does not use money. I have corncobs but want beadwork, while you have beadwork but want corncobs. We could barter corncobs for beadwork. People have been bartering for thousands of years and continue to do so today.

Bartering is a time-consuming practice. First, you must bargain and come to an agreement about what items are worth. How many corncobs should be traded for beadwork? Second, what if I require your beadwork, but you don't need my corncobs? We would have to find someone else who wants corncobs. She would need to have something you want—like milk. Then, I could give her the corncobs, she could give you her milk, and you could give me your beadwork. It's all very complicated!

Money

People had to come to an agreement on what possessions to trade when bartering. They traded items they all found useful. Many things were used as money.

Over time, people fashioned coins from metals. Metal coins were convenient as money because everyone agreed that metal was valuable. Metal coins are easy to carry, and they do not wear out or fall apart.

Money simplified trading. You don't want my corncobs, so I sell them to someone who does. I take money and give it to you for your beadwork. You can spend the money on anything you consider necessary.

69

Bills make carrying money easier because a single bill is worth several coins. It would be hard to carry a heavy container filled with coins all the time! Coins let us purchase things for less than $1.00. The U.S. dollar is divided into 100 cents, so if something costs 25 cents, we can pay with a dollar and get 75 cents back.

Markets

Markets are places where people go to trade. People have been frequenting markets for thousands of years. The first markets were held outside. The *agora* was a market in ancient Greece. Markets are a logical way to trade. People can browse, discover what is for sale, and then try to get the best deal for what they want.

Internet auction sites are also markets. You can research what is for sale. You can still attempt to get the best deal. But you do not have to walk around. You can conduct your shopping on a computer.

Think About It!

Besides using cash, what are some other ways people buy things today?

70

States of Matter

Matter can take many forms. It can be a solid, a liquid, or a gas. Each form does different things.

Solids

A solid can be hard or soft. It can be big or small. Wood is a solid. Plastic and metal are both solids. So are straw and sand. People can make solids. Solids that people make can be anything from computers to clothes. Ice is a common solid. It is the solid state of water. Things in a solid state don't change shape easily.

Liquids

Liquids do change shape. They can flow, pour, and even spill. They change shape to fill the space around them. Milk, oil, and ink are all liquids. Have you ever knocked over a cup of juice? It probably came out of the cup and spilled. It may have run off the table. This is because liquid flows freely. Water is the most common liquid on Earth. It doesn't have a shape. It takes the shape of what it is in. Water keeps flowing if there isn't something to hold it.

Gases

Gases don't have shapes or sizes of their own. They spread to fill the spaces they are in. Gases flow easily like liquids. But they can also be squeezed. This happens when you fill up some sports balls. Gas is forced into a small hole with a needle. When the needle is moved, the hole closes. Gas can only leave if the hole opens. Gases are often not visible. So most of the time, we can't see them. But gases are all around you. Even an empty glass is filled with air. The air we breathe is a mix of gases. One of the gases is oxygen.

Extend the Learning!

Many people think there are only three types of matter. But there are more! Plasma is the fourth form. It is like a gas. But magnets affect it. It is often very hot. It's the most common type of matter in space and on Earth. Plasma is found in our sun and the stars. It is also found in lighting. Even some TV screens use plasma. Scientists are always trying to find new ways to use plasma.

Think About It!
How would you define a solid, a liquid, and a gas?

States of Matter

Matter can take the form of a solid, a liquid, or a gas. Each state of matter has its own unique property.

Solids

Solids can be hard or soft. They can be big or small. Wood is solid matter. Plastic, metal, stone, bone, straw, sand, and crackers are all solids. Human-made solids include everything from computers to keys to the clothes you wear. Ice is a familiar solid. It is the solid state of water. Objects in a solid state don't change shape easily.

Liquids

Unlike solids, liquids do change shape. They can flow, pour, and even be spilled. They change their shape to fill the space around them. Milk, oil, and ink are all liquids. Have you ever accidentally knocked over a cup of juice? Most likely, it came flowing out of the cup and spilled all over the place. It may have run off the table and onto the floor. This is because liquid flows freely. Water is the most common liquid found on Earth. It doesn't have a definite shape, as ice has. Instead, it takes the shape of its container. If there isn't a container, water keeps flowing, just like the spilled juice. Water is made of the same molecules found in ice. But the molecules in water move more freely.

Gases

Gases don't have any shapes or sizes of their own. They spread quickly to fill the spaces around them. Similar to liquids, gases flow easily. But they can also be compressed, or squeezed. One example of compression is shown with a basketball. Gas is forced into a small hole in the ball with an inflator needle. When the needle is removed, the hole closes. Gas can only escape if the hole opens.

Gases are often invisible. So most of the time, we cannot see them. But gases are all around you. Even an empty glass is filled with air. The air we breathe in is a mixture of multiple gases. One of the gases is oxygen.

Extend the Learning!

Many people think there are only three states of matter. But there are actually more! Plasma is the fourth state of matter. It is similar to a gas, but magnets affect it. It is often very hot. It's actually the most common type of matter in the universe! Today, plasma is found in our sun, the stars, lightning, and even some TV screens. Scientists are always experimenting to find different ways to use plasma.

Think About It!

How are materials able to transform into different states of matter?

States of Matter

Matter can take the form of a solid, a liquid, or a gas. Each state of matter has its own unique set of properties.

Solids

Solids can be hard or soft, or they can be big or small. Wood is one example of solid matter. Plastic, metal, stone, bone, straw, sand, and crackers are all solids. Human-made solids include everything from computers to keys to the clothes you wear. Ice, the solid state of water, is a familiar solid. Objects in a solid state don't change shape easily.

Liquids

Unlike solids, liquids do change shape. They can flow, pour, and even be spilled. They change their shape to fill any space around them. Milk, oil, and ink are all liquids. Have you ever accidentally knocked over a cup of juice? Most likely, the juice came flowing out of the cup and spilled all over the place. It may have run off the table and onto the floor. This is because liquid flows freely unless it is stopped by a container or barrier. Water is the most common liquid found on Earth. It doesn't have a definite, stable shape as ice has. Instead, when it is located inside of something, it takes the shape of that container. If there isn't a container, water continues flowing, just like the spilled juice. Water is made of the same molecules found in ice but the molecules in water move more freely, while the molecules in ice move minimally.

Gases

Gases don't have any shapes or sizes of their own. They spread quickly to fill the spaces around them. Similar to liquids, gases flow easily. But they can also be compressed, or squeezed. One example of compression is shown in a basketball. Gas is forced into a small hole in the ball with an inflator needle. When the needle is removed, the hole closes—gas can only escape if the hole opens. Gases are often invisible. So, most of the time, we cannot see them. But gases are all around you; even an empty glass is filled with air. The air we breathe in is a mixture of multiple gases including oxygen.

Extend the Learning!

Many people think there are only three states of matter, but there are actually more! Plasma is the fourth state of matter. It is similar to a gas but is affected by magnets. It is often very hot. It's actually the most common type of matter in the universe! Today, plasma is found in our sun, the stars, lightning, and even some TV screens. Scientists are always experimenting to find different ways to use plasma.

Think About It!

Some solids seem to act like liquids. Sand, for instance, seems to do all of the things that liquid can do. How is this possible? What makes it a solid?

Phases of the Moon

Every day, the moon moves. Sunlight hits different parts of the moon as it rotates. Rotate means "to spin." The moon doesn't change shape. But it looks different to us. This is because we can only see the part that is lit by the sun. The other part is in the sun's shadow. It looks dark to us.

Long ago, people saw that the moon's shape made a pattern. The pattern lasted four weeks. They learned that the moon has eight phases. A phase is when the moon looks like it changes shape.

The first phase is the *new moon*. This is when the moon is between Earth and the sun. The side of the moon that faces us is in the shadows. We can't see it at all. The moon is closer to the sun in the sky. They rise and set at almost the same time.

The moon orbits Earth. After a few days, a tiny sliver of the moon shows. This phase is *waxing crescent*. Waxing means the moon looks like it's getting bigger. But the moon isn't really growing. Bit-by-bit, more of it is lit up each night.

The moon keeps revolving. We can see a bigger crescent. Soon we will see one half of the moon. This happens when the moon has traveled a quarter of its way around Earth. This phase is called the *waxing quarter*. You can see the moon for the first half of the night. But it sets before the sun rises. This leaves the sky dark early in the morning.

The next phase is called the *waxing gibbous*. The moon looks almost full. It can be seen in the sky most of the night.

Phases of the Moon

new moon   waxing crescent   waxing quarter   waxing gibbous

full moon   waning gibbous   waning quarter   waning crescent

     51630—Leveled Texts for Third Grade

Earth and the Moon

The moon keeps revolving. At last, we can see the *full moon*! During this phase, the moon will rise in the sky in the east. The sun sets in the west. The full moon will shine brightly all night. The full moon phase is the middle phase. Then the phases start over again. But now, they happen in reverse order. The moon will go through three more stages. At this time, the moon is waning. That means it looks smaller and smaller.

During the *waning gibbous*, the moon looks almost full. It is just missing a tiny sliver. Next is the *waning quarter*. We can see half of the moon lit up. The eighth phase is called *waning crescent*. We can only see a tiny sliver of the moon. Then the moon will return to the new moon phase. The moon has completed one full revolution around Earth. We will be able to see the new moon again a few days later. It will begin the waxing crescent phase again.

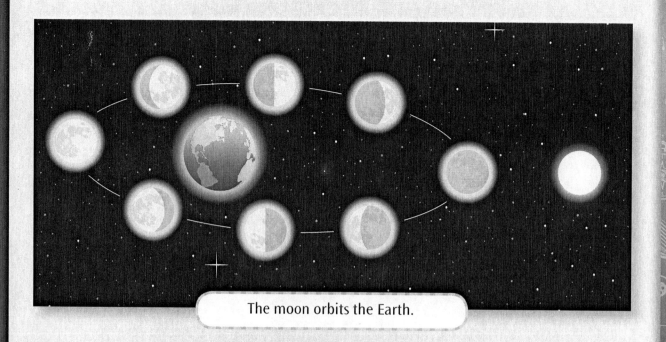

The moon orbits the Earth.

Think About It!
What are the phases of the moon?

Phases of the Moon

Each day of the month, the moon moves. Sunlight hits a different part of the moon as it rotates. The moon doesn't change shape, but it looks different to us on Earth. This is because we can only see the part that is lit by the sun. The other part of the moon is in the sun's shadow and appears dark to us.

People long ago noticed that the moon follows the same pattern every four weeks. They also learned that there are eight phases of the moon. A phase occurs each time the moon appears to change shape.

The first phase of the moon is called the *new moon*. This is when the moon is between Earth and the sun. The side of the moon that faces us is in the shadows, so we can't see it at all. During this phase, the moon is closer to the sun in the sky. The sun and moon rise and set at similar times.

The moon orbits Earth. After a few days, a tiny sliver of the moon begins to appear. This phase is called *waxing crescent*. The moon is said to be waxing when it appears to grow in the sky. Of course, the moon isn't actually growing. But, bit-by-bit, more of it is lit up each night.

As the moon travels around Earth, the part that we can see increases to a larger crescent shape. Soon we will see one half of the moon. This happens when the moon has finished a quarter of its revolution around Earth. This phase is called the *waxing quarter*. The moon will be visible for the first half of the night and will set early before the sun rises. This leaves the sky dark in the early morning hours.

The next phase is called the *waxing gibbous*. During this phase, the moon appears almost completely full and can be seen in the sky through most of the night.

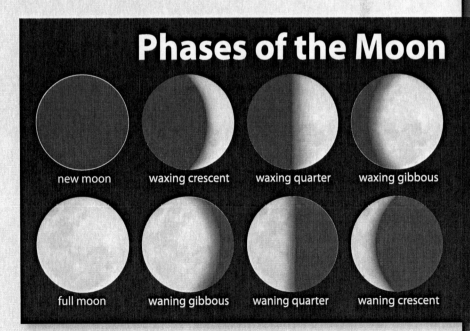

Phases of the Moon

new moon	waxing crescent	waxing quarter	waxing gibbous
full moon	waning gibbous	waning quarter	waning crescent

51630—Leveled Texts for Third Grade

Earth and the Moon

The moon continues to revolve around Earth. At last, we can see the *full moon*! During this phase, the moon will rise in the sky in the east while the sun sets in the west. The giant circle will shine brightly through the night. The full moon phase marks the halfway point in the moon's journey around Earth. Then, the phases start over again but in reverse order. The moon must make its way to the other side of its orbit. The moon will go through three more stages. It will appear to get smaller and smaller. At this time, the moon is said to be waning.

During the *waning gibbous*, the moon looks like a full moon minus a tiny sliver. Next is the *waning quarter* moon, when we can see half of the moon lit up. The eighth phase is called *waning crescent*. During this phase, we can only see a tiny sliver of the moon. Then the moon will return to the new moon phase. The moon has completed one full revolution around Earth. We will be able to see the moon again a few days later as it enters the waxing crescent phase again.

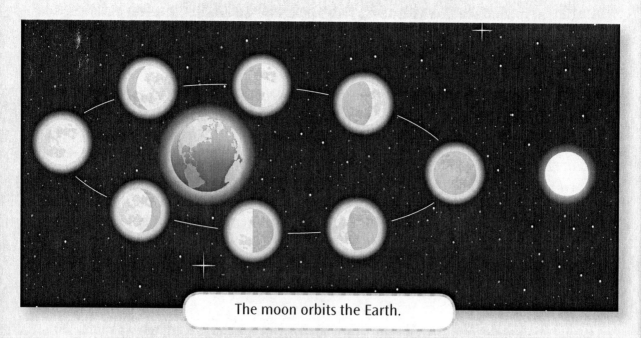

The moon orbits the Earth.

Think About It!
What is the difference between the waxing and waning phases?

Phases of the Moon

Each day of the month, the moon moves as it revolves around Earth. Sunlight hits a different part of the moon during its rotation. The moon doesn't change shape, but it looks different to us on Earth because we can only see the part that is lit by the sun. The other part of the moon is in the sun's shadow and appears dark to us.

People long ago noticed that the moon follows the same pattern every four weeks. They also learned that there are eight phases of the moon. A phase occurs each time the moon appears to change shape.

The first phase of the moon is called the *new moon*, when the moon is between Earth and the sun. The side of the moon that faces us is in the shadows, so we can't see it at all. During this phase, the moon is closer to the sun in the sky, and they rise and set at similar times.

The moon orbits Earth, and after a few days, a tiny sliver of the moon begins to appear. This phase is called *waxing crescent*. The moon is said to be waxing when it appears to grow in the sky. Of course, the moon isn't actually growing, but bit-by-bit, more of it is lit up each night.

As the moon revolves around Earth, the part that we can see increases to a larger crescent shape. Soon, we will see one half of the moon because the moon has finished a quarter of its revolution around Earth. This phase is called the *waxing quarter*. The moon will be visible for the first half of the night and will set early before the sun rises; this leaves the sky dark in the early morning hours.

The next phase is called the *waxing gibbous*. During this phase, the moon appears almost completely full and can be seen in the sky throughout most of the night.

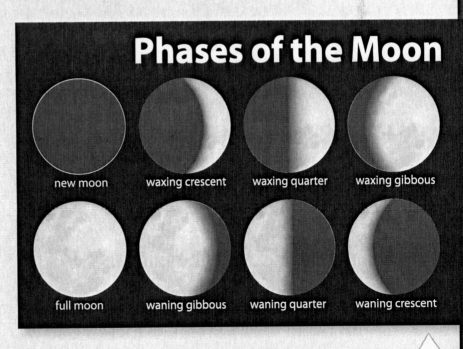

Phases of the Moon

new moon   waxing crescent   waxing quarter   waxing gibbous

full moon   waning gibbous   waning quarter   waning crescent

Earth and the Moon

The moon continues to revolve around Earth. At last, we can see the *full moon*, and the giant circle will shine brightly through the entire night. During this phase, the moon will rise in the sky in the east while the sun sets in the west. The full moon phase marks the halfway point in the moon's journey around Earth. After this phase, the other phases start over again but in reverse order. The moon must make its way to the other side of its orbit, and as it does, it will go through three more stages. It will appear to get smaller and smaller, so at this time, the moon is said to be waning.

During the *waning gibbous*, the moon looks like a full moon minus a tiny sliver. Next is the *waning quarter* moon, when we can see half of the moon lit up. The eighth phase is called *waning crescent*, when we can only see a tiny sliver of the moon. Then the moon will return to the new moon phase. The moon has completed one full revolution around Earth. We will be able to see the moon again a few days later as it enters the waxing crescent phase again.

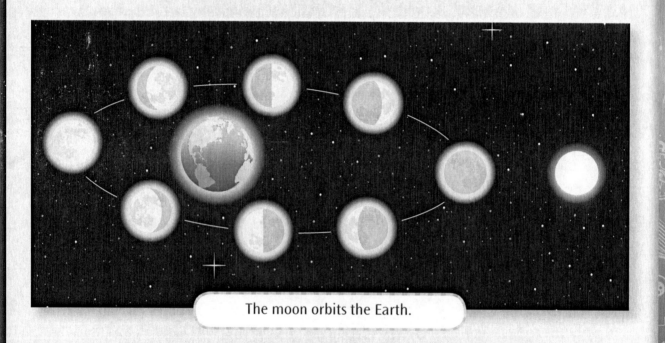

The moon orbits the Earth.

Think About It!

The first phase is referred to as the new moon.
Do you agree with this name? Why or why not?

Extreme Weather

Terrifying Tornadoes

Have you seen *The Wizard of Oz*? It is a movie. Dorothy has ruby red slippers. She has a little dog, too! Dorothy goes up in a tornado. It takes her to a new land. People like the movie. But it is not real life. Storms don't take you to fun places. If you see one, find shelter. They are not safe!

Tornadoes are strong winds. They are shaped like a funnel. They can start during bad weather. The wind moves around a spot. The wind goes as fast as 400 kilometers per hour! This is 250 miles per hour. The storms are like vacuums. They suck up things in their path. They can pick up cars. They toss them like toys. These storms tear houses apart. They destroy buildings. They are part of nature. But they are violent.

A man named Fujita studied tornadoes. He made a scale. It is called the Enhanced Fujita scale (EF). Many scientists use the scale. It rates storms. It measures damage. It also measures wind speed. The scale ranges from 0–5. A small storm is an EF0. The worst storm is an EF5.

May 22, 2011, was a sad day. There was an EF5 tornado. It hit Joplin, Missouri. It was a Sunday. The weather was humid and hot. No one knew what would happen. A huge twister came. It crushed homes. It ripped up streets. It sent objects flying. The storm was a mile wide! Over 100 people died. Many were hurt. There was over $2.1 billion in damage.

Horrendous Hurricanes

Hurricanes start as storms at sea. They can't hurt the sea. But the storms can move. Sometimes, they hit land. They can hurt land. These storms bring a lot of rain. They also bring strong winds.

Hurricanes start as tropical storms. The storm might reach 119 kph (73 mph). Then, it changes. It picks up warm water from the ocean. The water is vapor. This vapor makes clouds. The clouds make a spiral. An "eye" is in the center. The weather is calm there. Outside the eye, the weather is wild.

On October 29, 2012, there was a big storm. It was in New York and New Jersey. The beaches flooded. There were huge waves. Water poured into homes. Subways filled with water. That night, a hurricane hit land. It was Hurricane Sandy. The next day, people were upset. There were billions of dollars in damage. Millions of people did not have power. Thousands of people lost their homes. Many people died.

Hurricane Sandy was huge. It was one of the biggest storms ever. It affected more than 12 states. It also hit two other countries. There were strong winds and storm surges. They caused a lot of harm. New York and New Jersey were hit the hardest. But the people worked together. They fixed their homes. They rebuilt their stores. They helped others.

Think About It!

How is the tornado in *The Wizard of Oz* different from a real-life tornado?

Extreme Weather

Terrifying Tornadoes

Have you ever seen *The Wizard of Oz*? It's the movie about Dorothy and her ruby red slippers. She had a little dog, too! In the movie, Dorothy gets swept up in a tornado. It takes her to a magical land. This is a great movie. But it's not real life. Tornadoes don't whisk you away to exciting places. You should always seek shelter from tornadoes. They are not safe!

Tornadoes are funnels of strong wind. They occur during storms. The wind moves around a central point. The wind can reach speeds of over 400 kilometers per hour. This is 250 miles per hour. Tornadoes act like giant vacuums. They suck up things in their path. They can pick up cars and toss them like toys. Tornadoes tear houses apart. They destroy buildings. They are a violent force in nature.

Tetsuya Fujita is a tornado expert. The Fujita scale is named after him. Scientists use this scale. It rates tornadoes. It is based on the damage a tornado can cause. It also measures wind speed. The Enhanced Fujita scale (EF) ranges from 0–5. The low end of the scale is EF0. This is a small tornado. The worst tornado is an EF5.

On May 22, 2011, an EF5 tornado hit Joplin, Missouri. It was a Sunday afternoon. The weather was humid and hot. No one knew a tornado was coming. The huge twister flattened homes. It ripped up streets. It sent debris flying. At one point, the tornado was almost a mile wide! Over 100 people lost their lives. Many more were injured. There was over $2.1 billion in damage.

85

Horrendous Hurricanes

Hurricanes start at sea. There, they cause little damage. But the storms can hit land. Then, they are very destructive. Hurricanes bring heavy rain and strong winds.

Hurricanes begin as tropical storms. But when a storm reaches 119 kph (73 mph), it changes. It picks up warm water from the ocean. The water is in the form of vapor. This vapor forms clouds. The clouds form a spiral. An "eye" can be seen in the center of the hurricane. In the eye, the weather is calm. Outside the eye, the weather is chaotic.

On October 29, 2012, the coasts of New York and New Jersey began to flood. There were huge waves. Water poured into homes. Subways filled with water. That night, a hurricane came ashore. It was Hurricane Sandy. When the sun rose the next day, people were shocked. There were billions of dollars in damage. Millions of people did not have power. Thousands of people lost their homes. Many people lost their lives.

Hurricane Sandy was one of the biggest storms in history. It affected more than 12 states. It also hit the Caribbean and Canada. Strong winds and storm surges caused the most damage. New York and New Jersey were hit the hardest. But the people in these states worked together. They fixed their homes. They rebuilt their businesses. They helped one another.

Think About It!
What are some differences between hurricanes and tornadoes?

Extreme Weather

Terrifying Tornadoes

Have you ever seen *The Wizard of Oz*? It's the movie with Dorothy, her ruby red slippers, and her little dog, too! In the movie, Dorothy gets swept up in a tornado. It takes her to an enchanted land. While this may make for a great movie, in real life, tornadoes don't whisk you away to magical places. In fact, you should always seek shelter from tornadoes because they are dangerous!

Tornadoes are funnels of powerful wind that occur during thunderstorms. The wind moves around a central point. The wind can reach speeds of over 400 kilometers per hour (250 miles per hour). Tornadoes act like giant vacuums by sucking up everything in their path. They can pick up cars and toss them like toys. Tornadoes tear apart houses and can destroy buildings. They are one of the most violent forces in nature.

Tetsuya Fujita is a tornado expert. The Enhanced Fujita scale (EF) is named after him. Scientists around the world use this scale to rate tornadoes. It is based on the damage a tornado can cause. It also measures wind speed. The low end of the scale is EF0, which is a small tornado. The worst tornado is an EF5.

On May 22, 2011, an EF5 tornado hit Joplin, Missouri. It was a humid and hot Sunday afternoon. No one in Joplin knew that a powerful tornado was about to tear through the town. The massive twister flattened homes. It ripped up streets and sent debris flying. At one point, the tornado was almost a mile wide! Over 100 people lost their lives, and many more were injured. There was over $2.1 billion in damage.

Horrendous Hurricanes

When hurricanes are out at sea, they cause little damage. But when these storms hit land, they are very destructive. Hurricanes bring heavy rain and strong winds.

Hurricanes begin as tropical storms. But when a storm reaches 119 kph (73 mph), it changes. It begins to pick up warm water from the ocean. The water is in the form of vapor, which condenses to form clouds. The clouds form a spiral. An "eye" can be seen in the center of the hurricane. In the eye, the weather is calm, but outside the eye, the weather is chaotic.

On October 29, 2012, the coasts of New York and New Jersey began to flood. Huge waves pounded the shoreline. Water poured into homes, and subways filled with water. That night, a hurricane came ashore. It was Hurricane Sandy. When the sun rose the next day, people could not believe what they saw. There were billions of dollars in damage. Millions of people were without power, and thousands of people had lost their homes. Many people had lost their lives.

Hurricane Sandy was one of the biggest storms in history, affecting more than 12 states, the Caribbean, and Canada. Strong winds and storm surges caused the most damage. New York and New Jersey were hit the hardest, but the people in these states worked together. They fixed their homes and rebuilt their businesses. They helped one another.

Think About It!
What are key similarities between tornadoes and hurricanes?

Photosynthesis

Parts of a Plant

Plants can grow almost anywhere on Earth. They grow in the ocean. They grow in the mountains. They even grow in deserts! There are over 300,000 types of plants. Plants have features that help them live in these places. But all plants need the same things to live. They all need sun, water, air, and food.

Roots

Have you ever thought about why plants don't blow away when it's windy? Or have you thought about why they don't wash away when it's raining? It's because plants have strong and sturdy roots. Roots keep plants in the ground. They grow under the soil. Humans absorb the nutrients they need to live from food. But plants use their roots to absorb nutrients from the soil.

Different plants have different roots. Some plants have a *taproot* system. This means they have one big root. Little roots grow from it. This type of root can be very long. It lets the plant get water from deep under the soil. Large trees have a taproot system. Other plants have a *fibrous root* system. This means many thin roots grow from the plant's stem. These roots stay shallow. Garden plants usually have a fibrous root system.

Not all roots grow underground. Some rise from the stem. They can hang in the air. They can stretch through the air. Then they work their way underground. Corn has this type of root system.

Stems

Stems are strong. They have to be because they have an important job to do. Stems hold up and support the leaves and flowers of plants. They are the plant's backbone. As a plant gets older, the stem grows longer and thicker. The outside of the stem becomes rough. This is so it can protect the plant.

The inside of a stem is like a road system for plants. Tiny tubes carry water and nutrients through the plant. Stems also store nutrients for plants to use later.

Leaves

Have you ever gathered a big pile of leaves and then jumped into it? Have you made an art project with leaves? Leaves are beautiful. They are also an important part of every plant. There are many different types of leaves. Some are big, and some are small. Some are smooth and glossy. Others are rough and have jagged edges. Some are green. Others may be brown or orange.

Leaves are where plants make their food. It happens in the part of the leaf called the *blade*. The food moves through a leaf's veins to the stalk. The stalk is the part of a leaf that connects to the stem. All of these parts work together to help the plant grow big and strong.

Think About It!
What are the parts of a plant?

Photosynthesis

Parts of a Plant

Plants can grow almost anywhere on Earth. They grow in the ocean. They grow in the mountains. They even grow in deserts! There are 300,000 types of plants in our world. Plants have features that help them live in these places, but all plants rely on the same things to survive. They all need sun, water, air, and food; they also all have the same parts to help them live.

Roots

Have you ever thought about why plants don't blow away when it's windy? Or have you thought about why they don't wash away when it's raining? It's because plants have strong and sturdy roots. Roots anchor plants into the ground and grow underneath the soil. Humans absorb the nutrients they need to live and grow from food, but plants use their roots to absorb nutrients from the soil.

Different types of plants have different types of roots. Some plants have a *taproot* system, which means they have one big root from which little roots grow. This type of root can grow very long and lets the plant get water from deep under the soil. Large trees are an example of a plant with a taproot system. Other plants have a *fibrous root* system in which a bunch of thin roots grows from the stem of the plant. These roots typically stay shallow. Garden plants usually have a fibrous root system.

Not all roots grow underground. Some rise from the stem and hang in the air or stretch through the air before working their way underground. Corn has this type of root system.

Stems

Stems are strong because they have an important job to do. Stems hold up and support the leaves and flowers of plants, acting as the plant's backbone. As a plant gets older, the stem grows longer and thicker. The outside of the stem becomes rough so that it can protect the plant.

The inside of a stem acts as a road system for plants. Tiny tubes carry water and nutrients throughout the plant. Stems also store nutrients for plants to use later.

Leaves

Have you ever gathered a big pile of leaves and then jumped into it? Have you made an art project with leaves? Leaves are beautiful, but they are also an important part of every plant. There are many different types of leaves. Some are big, and some are small. Some are smooth and glossy. Others are rough and have jagged edges. Some are green, and others may be brown or orange.

Leaves make their food in the part of the leaf called the *blade*. The food then moves through a leaf's veins to the stalk. The stalk is the part of a leaf that connects to the stem. All of these parts work together to help the plant grow big and strong.

Think About It!
How do the parts of a plant work together to help it live?

Photosynthesis

Parts of a Plant

Plants can grow and flourish in almost every location on Earth. They grow in the depths of the oceans, in the heights of the mountains, and even in the parched deserts! There are over 300,000 varieties of plants on our planet. Plants have unique features that enable them to live in these diverse habitats, but all plants depend on the same things to survive: sun, water, air, and food. Additionally, they all have the same parts to help them thrive.

Roots

Have you ever pondered why plants don't blow away during strong winds? Or questioned why they don't wash away when it's raining? It's because plants have strong and sturdy roots. Roots anchor plants into the ground and grow underneath the soil. Similar to the way humans absorb the nutrients they need to live and grow from the foods they eat, plants use their roots to absorb essential nutrients from the soil.

Different types of plants have different roots. Some plants have a *taproot* system, which means they have one large root from which smaller roots grow. This type of root can grow to great lengths and allows the plant to retrieve water from deep beneath the soil. Large trees such as the oak and walnut have a taproot system. Other plants have a *fibrous root* system in which large amounts of thin roots grow from the stem of the plant. These roots typically stay shallow. Garden plants and grasses customarily have a fibrous root system.

Not all roots grow underground; some rise from the stem and hang in the air or stretch through the air before working their way underground. Corn is an example of this root system.

93

Stems

Stems are strong because they have a significant task. Stems hold up and support the leaves and flowers of plants, acting as the plant's backbone. As a plant matures, the stem grows longer and thicker. The outside of the stem becomes rough, which enables it to better protect the plant.

The interior of the stem acts as a road system. Minuscule tubes carry water and nutrients throughout the plant. Stems are also capable of storing nutrients for plants to use when necessary.

Leaves

Have you ever gathered a gigantic pile of leaves and then jumped into it? Have you ever made an art project with leaves? Leaves are beautiful, but they are also an important part of every plant. There are several different types of leaves. Some are large, and some are quite small. Some are smooth and glossy, while others are rough and have jagged edges. Some are green, and others may be brown or orange.

Plants create their nourishment in a part of the leaf called the *blade*. The food then travels through the leaf's veins to the stalk. The stalk is the part of a leaf that connects to the stem. All of these parts work together to help the plant grow healthy and strong.

Think About It!
What are two reasons stems grow longer and thicker as plants mature?

Gravity

Effects of Gravity

Everything on Earth attracts to everything else. Gravity affects all things. It even affects small bugs and big trucks! Life on Earth is used to gravity. Our bodies need it. We fight its pull. This keeps our bones and muscles strong. It helps carry blood in our bodies. But gravity does more. It affects the planet in big ways.

Rock Cycle

Rocks have been around for a long time. They seem hard to break. But rocks are always changing. This change is the rock cycle. Gravity causes change. Tiny grains of sand feel its effect. So do huge canyons.

Wind and water are hard at work. They break up big rocks. The rocks are now smaller. Gravity pulls loose rock to the ground. It pulls small rocks off cliffs. The pieces become tiny. Gravity pulls rocks into volcanoes. They go under the ground. Down below, there is heat. There is pressure. The rocks change. Now, they are a new kind of rock. The cycle keeps going.

Water Cycle

Water on Earth is very old. It is billions of years old! Gravity pulls on drops of rain. The water is reused. This happens over and over. It is the water cycle. Gravity is a big part of this cycle.

Gravity pulls water. It starts in clouds. Then, rain falls to the ground. Gravity pulls it down hills. Snow melts. Gravity pulls it down hills, too. It also pulls water through rocks and soil. Water goes deep in the ground. Plants use it to grow. The water keeps moving. It may form a pond, lake, or stream. Gravity pulls water downstream. It finally reaches the ocean. Water evaporates. It rises into the air. Then, the cycle begins again.

Tides

Have you seen the ocean? Sometimes, the water is high on the shore. This is called *high tide*. Other times it is different. You can see more of the shore. This is called *low tide*. The moon's gravity causes tides.

The moon's gravity pulls on Earth. It affects our oceans. It creates a bulge in the water. This happens on both sides of Earth. When the moon is overhead, it is high tide. The rotation of the Earth also affects tides. There are two high tides and two low tides each day.

high tide

low tide

Think About It!
How does gravity affect Earth?

Gravity

Effects of Gravity

Everything on Earth is attracted to everything else. Gravity affects all things, from small bugs to tall buildings. It helps life on Earth develop. It makes us feel comfortable. Our bodies fight the pull of gravity. This keeps our bones and muscles strong. Gravity even helps carry blood through our bodies. But gravity also affects the planet in bigger ways.

Rock Cycle

Rocks have been around forever. They may seem hard to destroy. But the rock cycle is always changing. Gravity is a force that causes change. Everything from a grain of sand to a huge canyon feels gravity's effects.

Wind and water break large rocks into small pieces. Gravity pulls loose rock to the ground. It pulls small rocks off a cliff. The rocks break into smaller pieces. Gravity pulls rocks into volcanoes. They also go under the ground. Below Earth's surface, there is heat and gravity. Rocks turn into new types of rocks. The cycle continues.

Water Cycle

Gravity pulls on tiny raindrops, too. The water on Earth is billions of years old. The water cycle reuses water. Gravity is important in this cycle.

Gravity pulls water from clouds to Earth. Raindrops land on the ground. Gravity pulls them downhill. When snow melts, it is pulled downhill by gravity. It also pulls water through layers of rocks and soil. Water goes deep into the ground. Plants use it to live and grow. The water keeps traveling. It may form ponds, lakes, or streams. Gravity pulls water downstream until it reaches the ocean. The water in oceans, ponds, and streams also evaporates. It rises into the air. Then, the cycle begins again.

Tides

Have you seen the ocean? Sometimes, the water is high on the shore. This is called *high tide*. Other times, the water seems to shrink. This is called *low tide*. More of the shore can be seen. The moon's gravity causes this motion.

The moon's gravity pulls on Earth. The water in our oceans is pulled, too. This pull creates a bulge in the water on both sides of the planet. When the moon is directly overhead, it is high tide. The moon's gravity and Earth's rotation create tides. There are two high tides and two low tides each day.

high tide

low tide

Think About It!
How does gravity affect the water cycle?

Gravity

Effects of Gravity

Everything on Earth is attracted to everything else—including Earth! Gravity affects everything from the smallest bug to the tallest skyscraper. Gravity has developed life on Earth in ways that make us feel comfortable. Fighting against the pull of gravity keeps our bones and muscles strong. Gravity even helps carry blood through our bodies. But gravity also affects the planet in bigger ways.

Rock Cycle

Rocks may seem like they have been around forever and are impossible to destroy. But they are constantly changing due to the rock cycle. Gravity is one of the forces that drive this change. Everything from a grain of sand to huge canyons feels gravity's effects.

Wind and water break large rocks into small pieces. Gravity pulls loose rock to the ground. If it pulls small rocks off a cliff, they will break into even smaller pieces. Gravity also pulls rocks into volcanoes and underground. Below Earth's surface, heat and gravity's pressure turn rocks into new types of rocks, and the cycle continues.

Water Cycle

Gravity pulls on large rocks and tiny raindrops, too. The water on Earth has been here for billions of years. The water cycle reuses this water every day. Gravity plays an important role in this cycle.

Gravity pulls water from clouds to Earth. When raindrops land on the ground, gravity pulls them downhill. When snow melts, it's also pulled downhill by gravity. Gravity also pulls water through layers of rocks and soil, deep into the ground. Plants use this water to live and grow. As water travels, it may form ponds, lakes, or streams. Gravity pulls water downstream until it reaches the ocean. The water in oceans, ponds, and streams also evaporates. It rises into the air. Then, the cycle begins again.

Tides

Have you ever been to the ocean? Sometimes, the water level is high on the shore. This is called *high tide*. At *low tide*, the water level seems to shrink, so more of the shore can be seen. The moon's gravity causes this mysterious motion.

The moon's gravity pulls Earth toward it. And the water in Earth's oceans is pulled, too. This pull creates a bulge in the water on both sides of the planet. When the moon is directly overhead, it is high tide. The moon's gravity and Earth's rotation create two high tides and two low tides each day.

high tide

low tide

Think About It!

Are the effects of gravity on the water cycle important? How would the water cycle be different without the effects caused by gravity?

Our Natural Resources

Essential Resources

There are many natural resources. Some we cannot live without. These are essential resources. We need these things to survive. They include water, land, and trees.

Water

Water is very important. We could not live without it. We need water to drink. It is a basic need for all people. But we can only drink freshwater. It must come from rivers and rainfall. Ocean water is too salty for us to drink.

Some plants give us food. They also need water. Long ago, farmers had to water their crops. They learned they could use rivers. So they dug trenches in the ground. Trenches are thin paths in the ground. They brought water from a river or stream to their fields. This is called *irrigation*.

Land

We need land for agriculture. This is farming. Farmers need land to grow crops. But they cannot grow crops on all land. The land needs healthy soil, or dirt. Land is a natural resource. It helps give us food.

Farmers grow corn, wheat, and other crops. These crops help feed people all around the world. Farmers also raise animals such as cows, chickens, and pigs. These animals give us milk, eggs, and meat. Farmers need land so they can raise animals.

Think of things we eat for breakfast. What if we didn't have chickens or cows? We would not have eggs or milk. What if we didn't have wheat? We would not have toast or cereal. Land gives us the food we need to live.

Trees

Trees are another natural resource. We could not live without them. The leaves on trees give us oxygen. We need oxygen to breathe.

Trees also give us food. Some trees make fruits or nuts. We can eat those things! Trees are used to make lumber. Lumber is made when trees are cut into boards. People use these boards. They can make houses, schools, and stores. Lumber is also used to make furniture. It can make tables and chairs. People can also use trees for firewood. This helps them keep warm.

It may seem like trees are everywhere. But our forests are disappearing fast! A person might cut down a tree. But they should plant a new one. This helps keep enough trees on Earth.

Think About It!
What are essential resources? What are natural resources?

Our Natural Resources

Essential Resources

There are some natural resources that we cannot live without. These are essential resources. We need these things to survive. They include things such as water, land, and trees.

Water

Water is one of our most important natural resources because we could not live without it. We need water to drink. It is a basic need for all human beings, but we can only drink freshwater that comes from rivers and rainfall. Ocean water is too salty for us to drink.

The plants that give us food also need water. Long ago, farmers learned that they could use rivers to water their crops. They dug trenches, or narrow paths, in the ground. The trenches brought water from a river or stream to their fields. This is called *irrigation*.

Land

We need land for agriculture, or farming. Farmers need plenty of land to grow crops. But they cannot grow crops on all kinds of land. They need land that has healthy soil, or dirt. Land is a natural resource that helps provide us with food.

Farmers grow corn, wheat, and many other crops. These crops help feed people all around the world. Farmers also raise animals such as cows, chickens, and pigs. These animals provide us with milk, eggs, and meat. Farmers need land to raise the animals.

Think of the things we eat for breakfast. Without chickens and cows, we would not have eggs or milk. Without wheat, we would not have toast or many breakfast cereals. Land gives us the food we need to live.

Trees

Trees are another natural resource that we could not live without. The leaves on trees give us oxygen, and we need oxygen to breathe.

Trees also give us food. Some trees make fruits or nuts that we can eat. Trees are also used to make lumber. Lumber is made when trees are cut into boards. People use these boards to make houses, schools, and other buildings. Lumber is also used to make furniture, such as tables and chairs. People can also use trees for firewood to keep warm.

It may seem like there are trees everywhere, but our forests are disappearing fast. This is one reason that people should plant a new tree if they cut one down. This helps keep enough trees on Earth.

Think About It!
Choose one essential resource.
Why is it important?

Our Natural Resources

Essential Resources

There are some natural resources that we cannot live without, called essential resources. We need these things to survive. These essential resources include water, land, and trees.

Water

Water is one of our most important natural resources because we cannot live without it. We need water to drink. It is a basic need for all human beings, but we can only drink freshwater that comes from rivers and rainfall because ocean water is too salty for people.

The plants that give us food also need water. Long ago, farmers learned they could use rivers to water their crops by digging trenches, or narrow paths, in the ground. The trenches brought water from a river or stream to the fields in a process called *irrigation*.

Land

We need land for agriculture, or farming. Farmers need an adequate amount of land to grow crops, but they cannot grow crops on every kind of land. They require land with healthy and fertile soil. Land is a natural resource that helps provide us with food.

Farmers grow corn, wheat, and many other crops, which help feed billions of people all around the world. Farmers also raise animals such as cows, chickens, and pigs. These animals provide us with milk, eggs, and meat. Farmers need land to raise the animals.

Think about the foods we eat for breakfast. Without chickens and cows, we would not have eggs or milk; without wheat, we would not have toast or many breakfast cereals. Land gives us the food we need to live.

Trees

Trees are another natural resource that we could not live without. The leaves on trees give us oxygen, and we need oxygen to breathe.

Trees also give us food. Some trees make fruits or nuts that we can eat. Trees are also used to make lumber, or trees cut into boards. Construction workers use these boards to build houses, schools, and other buildings. Carpenters use lumber to make furniture such as tables and chairs. People can also use trees for firewood to keep warm.

It may seem as if there are trees everywhere, but unfortunately, our forests are rapidly disappearing. This is one reason people should be responsible by planting a new tree if they cut one down. This helps keep plenty of trees on Earth.

Think About It!

If you had to rank the essential resources in order of importance, which one would top your list? Explain why.

The American Government

The Legislative Branch

This branch has two groups. One is the House of Representatives. It is called the House for short. The other is the Senate. Together, they form Congress. Congress has leaders from each state. They make laws.

The House is the larger group. Each state sends people to the House. Big states send more people. Small states send fewer people. So big states have more power.

The Senate also has leaders from every state. They each send two people. Every state has equal power.

The Executive Branch

The president leads this branch. He or she enforces laws. This is a big job. About four million people work for this branch!

The president runs America. He or she must follow the rules. The rules are in the U.S. Constitution. The president can't pass new laws alone. Congress has to create the laws. Then the laws can be passed. This is a rule.

Presidents represent America to the world. They travel a lot! They tour the world. Other leaders meet with them. They try to keep the peace. They make plans for the future.

The president works with Congress to make laws. Congress passes bills. This is an idea for a law. The president sees each bill. He or she might sign it. Then the bill is a law. But the president may choose not to sign it. Then, it is sent back to Congress. Maybe the bill needs to be changed. Or, the president may veto the bill. A *veto* means the bill is rejected. Vetoes keep Congress from having too much power. It is part of checks and balances.

The Judicial Branch

The Supreme Court leads this branch. It is the highest court in the country. It is in charge of all other courts. The Supreme Court hears the biggest cases in America. It listens to people who do not agree. It decides what laws mean. This is called a *ruling*. All courts must follow what the Supreme Court says. What it says becomes law.

The Supreme Court tries to treat all people fairly. Its judges have a special name. They are called *justices*. They hear about 100 cases a year. Their rulings are based on the laws.

The justices work hard. They protect people's rights. They look at laws. They make sure they are fair. It is their job to say how laws work. They might think that a law goes against the Constitution. Or they might think it is unfair. They can get rid of the law. They have the final say. Only one thing can change a ruling made by the Supreme Court. It is an amendment to the Constitution.

Think About It!

What does each branch of the government do?

The American Government

The Legislative Branch

The legislative branch is made up of two groups. One group is the House of Representatives, or simply the House. The other group is the Senate. Together, they are known as Congress. Congress is made up of leaders from each state. They make the laws.

The House is much larger than the Senate. Each state sends representatives to the House. Larger states send more people. Smaller states send fewer people. This means that bigger states have more power in the House.

Like the House, the Senate is made up of representatives from each state. But the Senate only has two members from each state. So, each state has the same power in the Senate.

The Executive Branch

The president leads the executive branch. He or she enforces laws. This is a big job. About four million people work for this branch!

The president makes sure the country runs smoothly. He or she must follow the rules in the U.S. Constitution. For example, the president cannot pass a new law alone. First, Congress has to agree that it should be a law. Then, it can be passed. This is a rule in the Constitution.

The presidents represent the country in world matters. This means that they travel a lot! They tour the world to meet with other leaders. They try to keep the peace. They make plans for the future.

The president works closely with Congress. Congress passes bills. Each bill then goes to the president. He or she may sign the bill. This makes the bill a law. The president can also send the bill back to Congress to be changed. Or the president may veto the bill. A *veto* means the bill is rejected. This keeps Congress from being too powerful. It is part of the checks-and-balances system.

109

The Judicial Branch

The Supreme Court leads the judicial branch. It is the highest court in the country. It is in charge of all the courts. The Supreme Court hears the biggest cases in America. It listens to people who do not agree on something. Then, it makes a decision about what the law means. This is called a *ruling*. All courts must follow what the Supreme Court says. Its rulings become the law.

The Supreme Court tries to treat all people fairly. The Supreme Court judges are called *justices*. They choose about 100 cases to hear each year. They make rulings based on the U.S. Constitution.

The Supreme Court justices work hard to protect people's rights. They look at laws to make sure they are fair. It is the job of the Supreme Court to say how the law works. If they think a law goes against the U.S. Constitution or is unfair, it is thrown out. They have the final say on the law. Only an amendment to the U.S. Constitution can change a ruling made by the Supreme Court. An amendment is a change to the U.S. Constitution.

Think About It!

How do Congress and the president work together to create laws?

The American Government

The Legislative Branch

The legislative branch is made up of two groups: the House of Representatives (or simply the House) and the Senate. Together, they are known as Congress and are made up of leaders from each state. The create laws for the United States.

The House is much larger than the Senate. Each of the fifty states sends representatives to the House. States with larger populations send more people, and states with smaller populations send fewer people. This means the more populous states have more power in the House.

Like the House, the Senate is made up of representatives from each state, but the Senate only has two members from each state. This means each state has the same power in the Senate.

The Executive Branch

The president is America's top leader and leads the executive branch. He or she enforces the laws. This is a big job—about four million people work for this branch!

The president makes sure the country runs smoothly. He or she must follow the rules in the U.S. Constitution. For example, the president cannot pass a new law alone. First, Congress has to agree that it should be a law, and then it can be passed. This is a rule in the Constitution.

Presidents represent America in world matters, so they travel a lot! They tour the world to meet with other leaders. They try to keep the peace and make plans for the future.

The president works closely with Congress. Congress passes bills, and each bill then goes to the president. He or she may sign the bill, which makes the bill a law. The president can also send the bill back to Congress to be changed, or the president may veto the bill. A *veto* means the bill is rejected. This keeps Congress from being too powerful. It is part of the checks-and-balances system.

111

The Judicial Branch

The Supreme Court leads the judicial branch. It is the highest court in the country and is in charge of all the courts. The Supreme Court hears the biggest cases in America. It listens to people who do not agree on something and then makes a decision, or ruling, about what the law means. All courts must follow what the Supreme Court says; its rulings become the law.

The Supreme Court tries to treat all people fairly. The Supreme Court judges are called *justices*. They choose about 100 cases to hear each year and make rulings based on the U.S. Constitution.

The Supreme Court justices work hard to protect people's rights as they look at laws to make sure they are fair. It is the job of the Supreme Court to say how the law works. If they think a law goes against the U.S. Constitution or is unfair, it is thrown out. They have the final say on the law. Only an amendment to the U.S. Constitution can change a ruling made by the Supreme Court. An amendment is a change to the U.S. Constitution.

Think About It!

The checks-and-balances system is used to keep each branch from getting too powerful. Do you think this is important? What might happen if this system did not exist?

America's Western Landmarks

Pearl Harbor

December 7, 1941, was a sad day. Japan bombed Pearl Harbor. This is in Hawaii. Over 2,000 people died. Many ships sank. One was the USS *Arizona*. This was during World War II.

People visit Pearl Harbor. They think about that sad day. They think of the brave soldiers. A memorial was built. This honors an event where many people died. This memorial is over a ship that sank. It is very long. It sags in the middle. The ends rise up. This was done on purpose. It is a symbol. Our country was strong. But it was weak for a short time. Then, it became strong again. Its name is World War II Valor in the Pacific. *Valor* means being brave. The soldiers who died were brave. They fought to protect our country.

Golden Gate Bridge

Many people felt it could not be done. But the Golden Gate Bridge was finished! It was May 27, 1937. The bridge is in San Francisco. This is in California. The bridge was hard to build. It had to cross a strait. A *strait* is a thin path of water. The strait has fog, winds, and tides. The bridge is between two bodies of water. One is the San Francisco Bay. The other is the Pacific Ocean.

The bridge is a suspension bridge. It hangs from cables. The cables are held up by towers. It took four years to build. The bridge is famous. It is known all over the world. It is painted orange. This was a special color. Orange is a warm color. It looks good with cool colors. Like blue water and skies! Plus, orange is easy for ships to see through fog.

The Hoover Dam

The Hoover Dam solved a problem. People lived out West. They had a concern. They wanted to control the Colorado River. The river starts in the Rocky Mountains. It flows to the Gulf of California. It carves out the Grand Canyon. But the river would flood. It did this every spring. Then, it

(113)

would be summer. The water would dry up. This hurt the people who lived in the West! People wanted to stop the floods. They wanted to store the water. It could be used during the dry summers.

In 1931 Herbert Hoover was president. He had a plan. He hired workers. They built a huge dam. A dam is a large wall. It slows down water. It can even stop it.

The dam worked! The floods stopped. Water was stored. It was used in summer. The dam uses water for energy. It turns water into power. The dam took five years to build. It still works today. It is a reminder. We can solve big problems. We just need to work as a team.

Taos Pueblo

Taos Pueblo is in New Mexico. It is an American Indian area. The Pueblo tribe lived there. A *pueblo* is a group of homes. They have many levels and rooms. The homes are made of adobe. This is like bricks. Straw, mud, and water make them. They dry in the sun. The pueblo was built a long time ago. More than 1,000 years! It is built close to a river. The river's name is the Rio Grande. The tribe wanted to live near the water. They could drink from the river. They could farm.

The pueblo is important. It shows how tribes lived long ago. The Pueblo tribe still lives there. They take care of the area. They welcome visitors. Guests can watch the tribe dance. They might be invited to a feast! This is a fun event.

Think About It!
What are landmarks? Why are they built?

America's Western Landmarks

Pearl Harbor

December 7, 1941, was a sad day. Japan bombed American ships. The ships were in Pearl Harbor, Hawaii. More than 2,000 people died that day. The USS *Arizona* sank. Many others ships also sank. This was during World War II.

Today, people visit Pearl Harbor. They think about the brave soldiers who died. The USS *Arizona* Memorial was built over the sunken ship. A memorial honors an event where many people died. This memorial is a long building. It sags down in the middle and rises up at both ends. This was done for a reason. It is a symbol that America was weak for a short time. But then it became strong again. Its name is World War II Valor in the Pacific. *Valor* means "bravery." The men and women who died were brave. They fought to protect our country.

Golden Gate Bridge

Many thought it could not be done. But the Golden Gate Bridge was completed on May 27, 1937. It is in San Francisco, California. It was a tough bridge to build. It had to cross a three-mile strait. A *strait* is a narrow path of water. It connects two larger bodies of water. They are the San Francisco Bay and the Pacific Ocean. This strait is known for its fog, winds, and tides.

The bridge is a suspension bridge. It is hung from cables. The cables are held up by towers. It took four years to build. The orange bridge is known all over the world. Its color was chosen for a reason. The warm color looks good against the cool colors of the water and sky. Plus, orange is easy for ships to see when there is heavy fog.

The Hoover Dam

The Hoover Dam was built for a purpose. People living in the West had a concern. They wanted to control the Colorado River. The mighty river starts in the Rocky Mountains. It flows to the Gulf of California.

115

It carves out the Grand Canyon. The problem was that the river caused big floods. This would happen in the spring. It would dry up in the summer. People wanted to stop the flooding. They also wanted to store the water. Then they could use it during dry summers.

In 1931, President Herbert Hoover had a plan. He hired many workers to build a huge dam. This is a large wall. It slows or stops the flow of water.

The dam worked! It stopped the river from flooding. It stored water for the summer months. The dam even took the energy of the flowing water. It turned the energy into electricity. The dam took five years to finish. It still works today. It reminds us that we can solve big problems. We just need to work together.

Taos Pueblo

Taos Pueblo is in New Mexico. It is an American Indian community. A pueblo is a set of homes. It is made of several stories of rooms. Stories are levels. The homes are built from adobe. This is a type of brick. They are made from straw, mud, and water. The bricks dry in the sun. The Pueblo tribe built the pueblo more than 1,000 years ago. They built it close to the Rio Grande River. They wanted to live near the water. The river gave them water to drink. It was also used for farming.

This is a key landmark. It shows how early American Indians lived. People of the Pueblo tribe still live there. They take care of the pueblo. They welcome visitors. Guests can watch American Indian dances. They might even be invited to join a family for a feast day!

Think About It!
Explain why each landmark was created.

America's Western Landmarks

Pearl Harbor

On December 7, 1941, Japan bombed American ships in Pearl Harbor, Hawaii. More than 2,000 people died that day. The USS *Arizona* was one ship that sank, but many others sank as well. This was during World War II.

Today, people visit Pearl Harbor and think about the brave soldiers who died there. A memorial was built over the sunken ship. It is called the USS *Arizona* Memorial. A memorial honors an event in which many people died. This memorial is a long building. It sags down in the middle and rises up at both ends. This was done because it is a symbol that America was weak for a short time, but then became strong again. It is called World War II Valor in the Pacific. *Valor* means bravery. The men and women who died were brave and fought to protect our country.

Golden Gate Bridge

Many thought it could not be done, but the Golden Gate Bridge was completed on May 27, 1937, in San Francisco, California. It was a tough bridge to build. It had to cross a three-mile strait. A *strait* is a narrow passage of water. It connects two larger bodies of water: the San Francisco Bay and the Pacific Ocean. This strait is known for its dense fog, gusty winds, and strong tides.

The bridge is a suspension bridge. This means the bridge is hung from cables that are held up by towers. It took four years to build. The orange bridge is known throughout the world, but its color was chosen for a reason. The warm color looks good against the cool colors of the water and sky. Plus, orange is easy for passing ships to see when there is heavy fog.

The Hoover Dam

The Hoover Dam was built because people living in the West had a concern. They wanted to find a way to control the Colorado River. The mighty river runs from the Rocky Mountains to the Gulf of California.

117

It is the river that carves out the Grand Canyon. The problem was that the river caused big floods in the spring and then it would dry up in the summer. People wanted to stop the flooding and store the water to use during dry summers.

In 1931, President Herbert Hoover hired many workers to build a huge dam. This is a large wall that slows or stops the flow of water.

The dam worked! It stopped the river from flooding. It also stored water for the summer months. The dam even took the energy of the flowing water and turned it into electricity. The dam took five years to finish and still works today. It reminds us that Americans can solve big problems by working together.

Taos Pueblo

Taos Pueblo is an American Indian community in New Mexico. A pueblo is a set of homes. It is made of several stories, or levels of rooms. The homes are built from adobe. This is a type of brick made from straw, mud, and water. The bricks are left out in the sun to dry. The Pueblo American Indians built the pueblo more than 1,000 years ago. They built it close to the Rio Grande River. They wanted to live near the water because the river gave them water to drink and to use for farming.

This is an important landmark. It shows us how early American Indians used to live. Members of the Pueblo tribe still live there. They take good care of the pueblo and welcome visitors. People can watch American Indian dances. They might even be invited to join a family for a feast day! This is a special day of eating and visiting.

Think About It!

Aside from the reasons above, what are some other reasons landmarks are built?

Doing Your Part

Ways to Help

People should help their community. It is part of being a good citizen. You can help others. You can keep your city clean. You can treat everyone fairly. These are all great ways to help!

Volunteer

People work hard. This makes their area better. The leaders do some of the work. But volunteers play a part, too. They work for free. They want to be good citizens.

Volunteers work. They do not get money. But they do get something in return. They make new friends. They learn how to do new things. They learn to be part of a team. And they help build better cities. It feels good to help others. You can volunteer. You can help make the world a better place.

Donate

Every place has people who need help. Maybe they lost their jobs. They may not have food or a home. Sometimes, people get very sick. They cannot take care of themselves. These people need help.

There are many ways to reach out to those in need. There are local charities. These are groups that help people. People can donate to these groups. *Donate* means to give. Some people donate money. The charities use it. They buy food, medicine, and clothes.

Some people donate items. They give clothing or food. Some charities take tables, toys, and books. They give these things to people who need them. Donating helps make a city stronger. It feels good to know you are helping people in need.

DONATION BOX

Each year, natural disasters happen. These are things like floods and fires. They can happen fast. There is often no warning. They leave many people in need. It is important for everyone to help when a disaster strikes.

Sometimes, people want to help. But they do not know how. They might want to donate food or clothing. But they do not know how to get things there. The people in need might be far away. Relief groups help. They get supplies to the people. The Red Cross is a relief group. It takes donations. Then, it gives them to people in need. The Red Cross even helps people in other countries.

Keep It Clean

Public places are areas that everyone can use. Have you ever run on a sandy beach? Or have you gone swimming in the ocean? Maybe you have hiked through a forest. Or you had a fun family picnic in a park. These are all public places. Public places are part of our communities. Everyone can enjoy them. It is important to keep them clean and safe.

Everyone can pitch in. This will help keep public spaces clean. Do not throw trash on the ground. This is breaking the law. Trash must be placed in a trash can. If you see trash on the ground, throw it away! Try to leave places looking better than they did when you got there.

Think About It!
What are some ways people can help their communities?

Doing Your Part

Ways to Help

Helping the community is part of being a good citizen. You can help people and keep your community clean. You can treat others fairly. These are all great ways to help!

Volunteer

People have to work hard to make their communities great. Community leaders do some of this work, but volunteers play a big part, too. This means they do the work for free. They do it because they want to be good citizens.

Volunteers do not get money for their work, but they do get something in return. They make new friends and learn how to do new things. They learn to be a part of a team and help build better communities. It feels good to help others. By volunteering, you can help make the world a better place.

Donate

Every community has people who need help. They may have lost their jobs. They may not be able to feed their families. They may not have a place to live. Sometimes, people get very sick. They may not be able to take care of themselves. These people need help.

There are many ways to reach out to those in need. There are local charities, which are groups that help people in need. People can donate, or give, to these charities. Some people donate money. The charities can use it to buy food, medicine, and clothing.

Some people donate items such as clothing or food. Some charities take furniture, toys, and books. They give these things to people who need them. Donating helps make a community stronger, and it feels good to know you are helping people in need.

DONATION BOX

Each year, natural disasters hit America. These are things such as floods and fires. These disasters can happen quickly. Sometimes, there is no warning. They leave lots of people in need. It is important for everyone to help when a disaster strikes.

Sometimes, people do not know how to help. They might want to donate food or clothing. But they may not know how to get things to people across the country. Relief groups work to get supplies to people who need them. The Red Cross is a relief group. It takes donations. Then, it gives them to people in need. The Red Cross even helps people in other countries.

Keep It Clean

Public places are areas that everyone can use. Have you ever built a sand castle on a beach or gone swimming in the ocean? Maybe you have hiked through a forest or had a fun family picnic in a park. These are all public places. Public places are a big part of communities. They are there for everyone to enjoy, so it is important to keep these public places clean and safe.

Everyone can pitch in and help keep public spaces clean. Do not throw trash on the ground. If you do, you are breaking the law. Trash must be placed in a trash can. If you see trash on the ground, throw it away! Try to leave places looking better than they did when you got there.

Think About It!
Why do people volunteer or donate to support their communities?

Doing Your Part

Ways to Help

Helping the community is part of being a good citizen. You can help people, keep your community clean, and treat others fairly. These are all fantastic ways to support your community!

Volunteer

People have to work hard to make their communities great. Community leaders do some of this work, but volunteers play an important part, too. This means they do the work for free because they want to be good citizens.

Volunteers do not get money for their work, but they do get something in return. They make new friends and learn how to do new things. They learn to be a part of a team and help build better communities. It feels good to help others. By volunteering, you can help make the world a better place.

Donate

Every community has people who need help. They may have lost their jobs, they may not be able to feed their families, or they may not have places to live. Sometimes, people get very sick and may not be able to take care of themselves. These people need assistance.

There are many ways to reach out to those in need. There are local charities, which are groups that help people in need. People can donate to these charities. Some people donate money, and then the charities can use it to purchase essential items like food, medicine, and clothing.

Some people donate tangible items such as clothing or food. Some charities take furniture, toys, and books. They give these things to people who need them. Donating helps make a community stronger, and it feels good to know you are helping people in need.

123

Each year, natural disasters hit America. These are things such as floods and fires. These disasters can happen quickly, often without any warning, and they leave many people in need. It is important for everyone to help when a disaster strikes.

Sometimes, people do not know how to help. They might want to donate food or clothing, but they may not know how to get supplies to people across the country. Relief groups work to get supplies to people who need them. The Red Cross is an example of a relief group. It takes donations and it gives them to people in need. The Red Cross even helps people in other countries.

Keep It Clean

Public places are areas that everyone can use. Have you ever built a sand castle on a beach or gone swimming in the ocean? Maybe you have hiked through a forest or had a fun family picnic in a park. These are all public places, which are a big part of communities. They are there for everyone to enjoy, so it is important to keep these public places clean and safe.

Everyone can pitch in and help keep public spaces clean. Do not throw trash on the ground, because if you do, you are breaking the law. Trash must be placed in a trash can, so if you see trash on the ground, throw it away! Try to leave places looking better than they did when you arrived.

Think About It!
Make a list of some other ways people can help their communities.

America's National Capital

Government Buildings

Washington, DC, is a big city. It has many buildings. The White House is one. The Capitol is another. The Supreme Court is a third. Leaders meet there. They make big decisions. Their choices affect the country.

The White House

The president lives in a special place. It is called the White House. He or she also works there. George Washington chose the place. This was in 1791. It took eight years to build. John Adams was the first person to live there. Later, it was the War of 1812. The British came. They set the White House on fire. It took years to fix. During the 1900s, the house changed. Many updates were made.

The White House has more than 130 rooms! Some rooms are named for their color. There is the Blue Room. There is the Green Room. And there is the Red Room. They are all famous. There are bedrooms. The president's family lives in them. There is also a big kitchen. The staff makes dinner. They can feed over 140 guests! There is a map room. There is a library. And of course, there are offices. People work there.

Outside, there is a pool. And there is a tennis court! These help the president stay fit. There is a place to practice golf. There are gardens. They have fresh vegetables. These help the president eat healthy.

The Capitol Building

Many people are in Congress. They work at the Capitol. It is in the center of the city. It stands for democracy. America believes all people should be free. They can make choices. Not like when there is a king or queen! All people have a say. They can be part of the country.

Building the Capitol was not easy. There was not enough money. They needed more space. The Capitol was built long ago. It is more than 200 years old. It has had many changes. It even caught on fire! Today, people visit this place. They want to see a statue. It sits on top of the building. It is named *Freedom*.

The Supreme Court

The Supreme Court began in 1790. But there was no building. This went on for a long time. It got one 145 years later. It is near the Capitol.

The courthouse stands tall. It has words carved on it. They read "Equal Justice Under Law." This reminds the justices to be fair. The Supreme Court is a good place. Each person can be heard.

People like to watch the cases. But finding a seat is hard! It can be very crowded. Some people wait all night. They can't wait to see the decision.

Think About It!
Why are these three government buildings important?

America's National Capital

Government Buildings

Washington, DC, has many government buildings. American leaders meet in them. They make big decisions for the country. The White House, the Capitol building, and the Supreme Court are three of these buildings.

The White House

The White House is where the president lives and works. In 1791, George Washington chose its place. It took eight years to build. John Adams was the first president to live there. During the War of 1812, the British came. They set the White House on fire. It took years to rebuild. During the 1900s, many updates were made to the house.

The White House has more than 130 rooms! Many of the rooms are known by their color. The Blue Room, the Green Room, and the Red Room are all famous rooms. There are bedrooms for the president's family. There is also a large kitchen. The staff can make dinner for over 140 guests! There is a map room and a library. And, of course, there are offices for people to work.

Outside, there is a swimming pool. There is a tennis court, too! These help the president stay fit. There is even a putting green to practice golf! There are also vegetable gardens. These help the president eat healthy.

127

The Capitol Building

Congress works in the Capitol building. It is in the center of the city. It is a symbol of democracy. This is an American value. It means that everyone should be free to make choices. A king or queen should not make them. Every citizen should get a say in how the country is run.

Building the Capitol was not easy. At times, there was not enough money. Other times, they needed more space. The Capitol building is more than 200 years old. It has survived many changes—even a fire! Today, many people come to admire the statue. It sits on top of the Capitol. It is named *Freedom*.

The Supreme Court

The Supreme Court began in 1790. But it took 145 more years for it to get its own building. Today, it is near the Capitol building.

The front of the courthouse has words carved above it. They read "Equal Justice Under Law." This reminds the justices to always be fair. The Supreme Court is a place where anyone can be heard.

People can watch court cases. But finding a seat is hard! Most of the cases are very crowded. Some people wait overnight to watch decisions be made.

Think About It!
The article says the Capitol building is "a symbol of democracy." What do you think this means?

America's National Capital

Government Buildings

Washington, DC, is home to many government buildings. American leaders meet in them to make big decisions for the country. The White House, the Capitol building, and the Supreme Court are three of these buildings.

The White House

The White House is where the president lives and works. In 1791, President Washington chose the site for the White House. It took eight years to build. John Adams was the first president to live there. During the War of 1812, the British set fire to the White House. It took years to rebuild. During the 1900s, many renovations were made to the house.

The White House has more than 130 rooms! Many of the rooms in the White House are known by their color. The Blue Room, the Green Room, and the Red Room are all famous rooms in the White House. There are bedrooms for the president's family. There is also a large kitchen where the staff can make dinner for over 140 guests! There is a map room, a library, and, of course, there are offices where people can work.

Outside, there is a swimming pool and a tennis court to help the president stay fit. There is even a putting green for the president to practice golf! There are also vegetable gardens to help the president eat healthy.

129

The Capitol Building

Congress works in the Capitol building in the center of the city. It is a symbol of democracy, an American value. It means that everyone should be free to make decisions. A king or queen should not make decisions for citizens; everyone should get a say in how the country is run.

Building the Capitol was not easy. At times, there was not enough money, and other times, they needed more space. The Capitol building is more than 200 years old. It has survived many changes—even a fire! Today, many people come to admire the statue named *Freedom,* which sits on top of the building.

The Supreme Court

The Supreme Court began in 1790, but it took 145 more years for it to get its own building. Today, it is located near the Capitol building.

The front of the courthouse has words carved above it reading "Equal Justice Under Law." This reminds the justices to always be fair. It promises that the Supreme Court is a place where anyone can be heard.

People are welcome to watch court cases, but finding a seat can be very difficult! Most of the cases are often very crowded. Some people wait overnight to watch decisions be made.

Think About It!

What saying or words would you choose to represent the White House? Why did you choose this?

References Cited

August, Diane, and Timothy Shanahan. 2006. *Developing Literacy in Second-Language Learners: Report of the National Literacy Panel on Language-Minority Children and Youth.* Mahwah, New Jersey: Lawrence Erlbaum Associates, Inc.

Fountas, Irene, and Gay Su Pinnell. 2012. *The Critical Role of Text Complexity in Teaching Children to Read.* Portsmouth, Virginia: Heinemann.

Tomlinson, Carol Ann. 2014. *The Differentiated Classroom. Responding to the Needs of All Learners, 2nd Edition.* Reston, Virginia: Association for Supervision and Curriculum Development.

Van Tassel-Baska, Joyce. 2003. "Differentiating the Language Arts for High Ability Learners, K–8. ERIC Digest." Arlington, Virginia: ERIC Clearinghouse on Disabilities and Gifted Education.

Vygotsky, Lev Semenovich. 1978. "Interaction Between Learning and Development." In *Mind in Society*, 79–91. Cambridge, Massachusetts: Harvard University Press.

Strategies for Using the Leveled Texts

Throughout this section are differentiation strategies that can be used with each leveled text to support reading comprehension for the students in your classroom.

Below-Grade-Level Students

KWL Charts

KWL charts empower students to take ownership of their learning. This strategy can be used as a pre- or post-reading organizer and a tool for further exploration or research on a topic. Guide students with the following questions:

- What can scanning the text tell you about the text?
- What do you know about the topic of this text?
- What do you want to know about this text?
- What did you learn about the topic?
- What do you still want to know about the topic? (*extension question*)

What do you KNOW?	What do you WANT to know?	What did you LEARN?

Strategies for Using the Leveled Texts *(cont.)*

Below-Grade-Level Students *(cont.)*

Vocabulary Scavenger Hunt

Another prereading strategy is a Vocabulary Scavenger Hunt. Students preview the text and highlight unknown words. Students then write the words on specially divided pages. The pages are divided into quarters with the following headings: *Definition*, *Sentence*, *Examples*, and *Nonexamples*. A section called *Picture* is put over the middle of the chart. As an alternative, teachers can give students selected words from the text and have them fill in the chart individually. (Sample words can be found on page 134.)

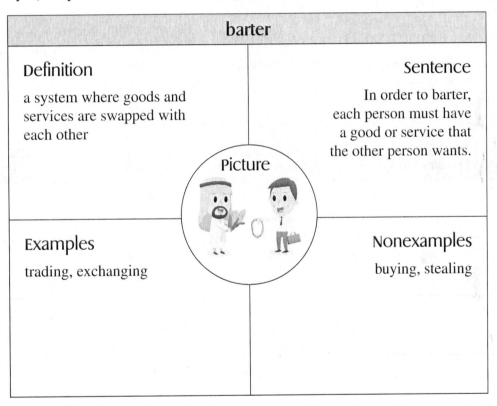

This encounter with new vocabulary words enables students to use the words properly. The definition identifies the word's meaning in student-friendly language, which can be constructed by the teacher and/or student. The sentence should be written so that the word is used in context. This sentence can be either one students make up or copied from the text in which the word is found. This helps students make connections with background knowledge. Illustrating the word gives a visual clue. Examples help students prepare for factual questions from the teacher or on standardized assessments. Nonexamples help students prepare for *not* and *except for* test questions such as "All of these are examples of bartering *except for* . . ." and "Which of these examples are *not* bartering?" Any information students are not able to record before reading can be added after reading the text.

Strategies for Using the Leveled Texts (cont.)

Below-Grade-Level Students (cont.)

Frontloading Vocabulary and Content

As an alternative to the Vocabulary Scavenger Hunt, teachers can frontload, or pre-teach, vocabulary or content in a text prior to reading. This can be a useful tool for all students, especially below-grade-level students, who struggle with on-demand reading and comprehension tasks. Activate students' prior knowledge by asking:

- What do you know about the word/topic . . .

- All these words are about the text you are going to read. Based on these words, what do you think the text will be about?

The words below can be used during frontloading discussions before reading a text. (Note: Some words are not found in all levels but can be used to focus students' attention toward the theme and main idea of text they will read.)

Text	Words, Themes, and Content
A Day in the Life of a Cowhand	cowhand, cattle, range, stampede, cattle drive
Sweet: Inside a Bakery	batter, ingredients, artist, hobby, icing
The Mystery of the Grand Bazaar	market, bazaar, merchants, deserted
How to Survive in the Jungle by the Person Who Knows	camouflage, fierce, coated, elementary, ravenous
Race to the Moon	junk, marvelous, unison, assembling, possessions
Our Vacation Budget	budget, expenses, unexpected, savings, allowance
Measuring Time	disqualified, digital, meter, accurate, tenth, hundredth
Natural Measures	volume, carat, cubit, sundial, volume, standard
My Lemonade Stand	income, profit, supplies, stretched, borrowed
The World of Trade	trade, goods, service, bartering, efficient, bargain
States of Matter	solid, liquid, gas, plasma, magnet
Phases of the Moon	phase, crescent, waxing, gibbous, waning, quarter
Extreme Weather	vapor, chaotic, funnels, tornado, hurricane
Photosynthesis	photosynthesis, fibrous, taproot, veins, blade, nutrients, flourish, nourishment
Gravity	gravity, cycle, high tide, low tide, evaporate
Our Natural Resources	natural, resource, essential, irrigation, agriculture, trench
The American Government	legislative, executive, judicial, Constitution, Congress, bill, law
America's Western Landmarks	landmark, symbol, memorial, valor, dam, pueblo
Doing Your Part	citizen, volunteer, donate, relief, charities, essential, tangible
America's National Capital	government, Capitol, Supreme Court, democracy

Strategies for Using the Leveled Texts (cont.)

Below-Grade-Level Students (cont.)

Graphic Organizers to Find Similarities and Differences

Setting a purpose for reading content focuses the learner. One purpose for reading can be to identify similarities and differences. This skill must be directly taught, modeled, and applied. Many of the comprehension questions in this book ask students to compare and contrast. The chart below can be used to respond to these questions.

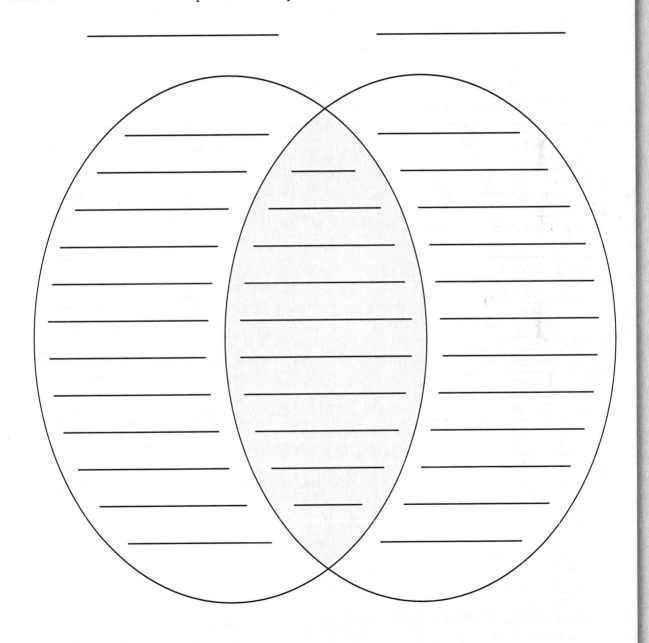

Strategies for Using the Leveled Texts *(cont.)*

Below-Grade-Level Students *(cont.)*

Framed Outline

This is an underused technique that yields great results. Many below-grade-level students struggle with reading comprehension. They need a framework to help them attack the text and gain confidence in comprehending the material. Once students gain confidence and learn how to locate factual information, the teacher can phase out this technique.

There are two steps to successfully using this technique. First, the teacher writes cloze sentences. Second, the students complete the cloze activity and write summary sentences.

Example Framed Outline

Before money was invented, people _____ and _____ for goods and _____. Later, when coins were invented, people used these _____ coins because they made trading _____. _____ are places where people can trade.

Summary Sentences

A long time ago people bartered to get things that they needed. Later, coins were made. When carrying large quantities of coins became troublesome, paper money was invented.

Modeling Written Responses

A frequent concern of educators is that below-grade-level students write poor responses to content-area questions. This problem can be remedied if resource teachers and classroom teachers model what good answers look like. This is a technique you may want to use before asking your students to respond to the comprehension questions associated with the leveled texts in this series.

First, read the question aloud. Then display the question on the board and discuss how you would go about answering the question. Next, write the answer using a complete sentence that accurately answers the question. Repeat the procedure for several questions so that students can understand that written responses are your expectation. To take this one step further, post a variety of responses to a single question. Ask students to identify the strongest response and tell why it is strong. Have students identify the weakest answers and tell why they are weak. By doing this, you are helping students evaluate and strengthen their own written responses.

Strategies for Using the Leveled Texts *(cont.)*

On-Grade-Level Students

Student-Directed Learning

Because they are academically on grade level, student-directed learning activities can serve as a way to build independence and challenge this population of students toward further success. Remember to use the texts in this book as jump starts so that students will be interested in finding out more about the topics. On-grade-level students may enjoy any of the following activities:

- Write your own questions, exchange them with others, and grade each other's responses.

- Review the text and teach the topic to another group of students.

- Read other texts about the topic to further expand your knowledge.

- Create an illustrated timeline or presentation on the topic to present to the class.

- Create your own story similar to the plot in the passage read.

- Lead a discussion group around the leveled question that accompanies the text.

- Research topics from the text in depth and write a new text based on the information.

- Extend the plot of the story or write a new ending to the text.

Highlight It!

Teach students to parse out information based on the genre while they are reading. Use the chart below and a highlighter to focus students on genre-specific text features.

Genre	What do I highlight?
fiction—historical fiction, realistic fiction, literature	characters problem setting solution theme/moral
nonfiction—biography, autobiography, informational	leading/main idea sentence important information sequence of events

Strategies for Using the Leveled Texts *(cont.)*

On-Grade-Level Students *(cont.)*

Detective Work

Teach students to be analytical, like detectives. Direct students' attention to text features such as titles, illustrations, and subheadings by asking students to cover the text and only look at the text features. They can use the chart below to organize analytical thinking about text features prior to reading the text.

Name of Text:		
Text Feature	Why do you think this feature was included?	What can this feature tell you about what the text might be about?
title, subtitle, and headings		
pictures, images, and captions		
diagrams and maps		

Strategies for Using the Leveled Texts *(cont.)*

Above-Grade-Level Students

Open-Ended Questions and Activities

Teachers need to be aware of activities that provide a ceiling that is too low for above-grade-level students. When given activities like this, these students become disengaged. These students can do more, but how much more? Offering open-ended questions and activities will provide above-grade-level students with opportunities to perform at or above their ability levels. For example, ask students to evaluate major events described in the texts, such as: "In what ways are the three states of matter similar?" or "Explain why checks and balances are important for all citizens." These questions require students to form opinions, think deeply about the issues, and form statements in their minds. Questions like this have lots of right answers.

The generic open-ended question stems listed here can be adapted to any topic. There is one leveled comprehension question for each text in this book. These extension question stems can be used to develop further comprehension questions for the leveled texts.

- In what ways did . . .
- How might you have done this differently . . .
- What if . . .
- What are some possible explanations for . . .
- How does this affect . . .
- Explain several reasons why . . .
- What problems does this create . . .
- Describe the ways . . .
- What is the best . . .

- What is the worst . . .
- What is the likelihood . . .
- Predict the outcome . . .
- Form a hypothesis . . .
- What are three ways to classify . . .
- Support your reason . . .
- Compare this to modern times . . .
- Make a plan for . . .
- Propose a solution to. . .
- What is an alternative to . . .

139

Strategies for Using the Leveled Texts *(cont.)*

Above-Grade-Level Students *(cont.)*

Tiered Assignments

Teachers can differentiate lessons by using tiered assignments or extension activities. These assignments are designed to have varied levels of depth, complexity, and abstractness. All students work toward one concept or outcome, but the lesson is tiered to allow for different levels of readiness and performance levels. As students work, they build on and extend their prior knowledge and understanding. Guidelines for writing tiered lessons include the following:

1. Pick the skill, concept, or generalization that needs to be learned.
2. Assess the students using classroom discussions, quizzes, tests, or journal entries.
3. Think of an on-grade level activity that teaches this skill, concept, or generalization.
4. Take another look at the activity from Step 3. Modify this activity to meet the needs of the below-grade-level and above-grade-level learners. Add complexity and depth for the above-grade-level learners. Add vocabulary support and concrete examples for the below-grade-level students.

Extension Activities Ideas

Extension activities can be used to extend the reading beyond the passages in this book. These suggested activities will help get you started. (Note: All the passages do not have extension activities.)

1. Pretend you own a bakery in your neighborhood. Create a menu detailing all of the options for your shop. Be sure to include the ingredients and price of each item.
2. Research wilderness survival and put together a brochure explaining things to bring, what to do, and what not to do to survive in the wilderness.
3. Help your parents plan a family vacation. In your plans, make sure to include how much the trip will cost and ways in which you plan to help save for the trip.
4. If cups come in packages of 25, and cost $5.00 each, how much money did he make on days 2–4? Make a chart to show how much money the lemonade stand made each day.
5. Like water, there are many things that we encounter on a daily basis that can be a solid, liquid, and/or gas. Create a triple Venn diagram and think of other things that fit into each category. Try to include at least three items in each part of the diagram.
6. What should you do in the case of extreme weather? Create a poster detailing the steps people should take in case of extreme weather. Be sure to include what people should do before to prepare for each scenario.
7. Our natural resources are being depleted every day. Write an opinion piece to your government explaining the importance of caring for each natural resource. Be sure to include ideas on how the government can help in your plans.
8. How can you and your friends "Do Your Part"? Make a list of the ways you, your friends, and/or family can help the community that you live in or your school.

140

Strategies for Using the Leveled Texts (cont.)

English Language Learners

Effective teaching for English language learners requires effective planning. To achieve success, teachers need to understand and use a conceptual framework to help them plan lessons and units. These are the six major components to any framework:

1. **Select and Define Concepts and Language Objectives**—Before having students read one of the texts in this book, first choose a subject/concept and a language objective (listening, speaking, reading, or writing) appropriate for the grade level. The next step is to clearly define the concept to be taught. This requires knowledge of the subject matter, alignment with local and state objectives, and careful formulation of a statement that defines the concept. This concept represents the overarching idea and should be posted in a visible place in the classroom.

   By the definition of the concept, post a set of key language objectives. Based on the content and language objectives, select essential vocabulary from the text. (A list of possible words can be found on page 134.) The number of new words selected should be based on students' English language levels. Post these words on a word wall that may be arranged alphabetically or by themes.

2. **Build Background Knowledge**—Some English language learners may have a lot of knowledge in their native language, while others may have little or no knowledge. Build the background knowledge of the students using different strategies, such as the following:

   Visuals—Use posters, photographs, postcards, newspapers, magazines, drawings, and video clips of the topic you are presenting. The texts in this series include multiple images, maps, diagrams, charts, tables, and illustrations for your use.

   Realia—Bring real-life objects to the classroom. If you are teaching units of measurement, bring in items such as scales or measuring cups.

   Vocabulary and Word Wall—Introduce key vocabulary in context. Create families of words. Have students draw pictures that illustrate the words and write sentences about the words. Also be sure you have posted the words on a word wall in your classroom. (Key vocabulary from the various texts can be found on page 134.)

   Desk Dictionaries—Have students create their own desk dictionaries using index cards. On one side of each card, they should draw a picture of the word. On the opposite side, they should write the word in their own language and in English.

Strategies for Using the Leveled Texts *(cont.)*

English Language Learners *(cont.)*

3. **Teach Concepts and Language Objectives**—Present content and language objectives clearly. Engage students by using a hook and pace the delivery of instruction, taking into consideration the students' English language levels. State the concept or concepts to be taught clearly. Use the first languages of the students whenever possible, or assign other students who speak the same languages to mentor and to work cooperatively with the English language learners.

   Lev Semenovich Vygotsky (1978), a Russian psychologist, wrote about the zone of proximal development. This theory states that good instruction must fill the gap that exists between the present knowledge of a child and the child's potential. Scaffolding instruction is an important component when planning and teaching lessons. English language learners cannot skip stages of language and content development. You must determine where the students are in the learning process and teach to the next level using several small steps to get to the desired outcome. With the leveled texts in this series and periodic assessment of students' language levels, you can support students as they climb the academic ladder.

4. **Practice Concepts and Language Objectives**—English language learners need to practice what they learn by using engaging activities. Most people retain knowledge best after applying what they learn to their own lives. This is definitely true for English language learners. Students can apply content and language knowledge by creating projects, stories, skits, poems, or artifacts that show what they have learned. Some activities should be geared to the right side of the brain, like those listed above. For students who are left-brain dominant, activities such as defining words and concepts, using graphic organizers, and explaining procedures should be developed. The following teaching strategies are effective in helping students practice both language and content:

   Simulations—Students re-create concepts in texts by becoming a part of them. They have to make decisions as if they lived in historical times. For example, students can pretend that they are representatives in Congress. They have to describe and act out how to pass a bill into a law. Or, students can act out a fictional passage. They can reenact the passage while extending their understanding of the main character's personality.

   Literature response—Read a text from this book. Have students choose two people described or introduced in the text. Ask students to write conversations the people might have. Or you can have students write journal entries about events in the daily lives of the important people. Literature responses can also include student opinions, reactions, and questions about texts.

Strategies for Using the Leveled Texts *(cont.)*

English Language Learners *(cont.)*

4. Practice Concepts and Language Objectives *(cont.)*

Have a short debate—Make a statement such as, "Metric is better than standard measurements." After reading a text in this book, have students think about the question and take positions based on their points of view. As students present their ideas, you or a student can act as the moderator.

Interview—Students may interview a member of their family or a neighbor to obtain information regarding a topic from the texts in this book. For example: How is your life similar to the lives of senators?

5. Evaluation and Alternative Assessments—Evaluation should be used to inform instruction. Students must have opportunities to show their understandings of concepts in different ways and not only through standard assessments. Use both formative and summative assessments to ensure that you are effectively meeting your content and language objectives. Formative assessment is used to plan effective lessons for particular groups of students. Summative assessment is used to find out how much the students have learned. Other authentic assessments that show day-to-day progress are: text retelling, teacher rating scales, student self-evaluations, cloze statements, holistic scoring of writing samples, performance assessments, and portfolios. Periodically assessing student learning will help you ensure that students continue to receive the correct levels of texts.

6. Home/School Connection—The home/school connection is an important component in the learning process for English language learners. Parents are the first teachers, and they establish expectations for their children. These expectations help shape the behavior of their children. By asking parents to be active participants in the education of their children, students get double doses of support and encouragement. As a result, families become partners in the education of their children and chances for success in your classroom increase.

You can send home copies of the texts in this series for parents to read with their children. You can even send multiple levels to meet the needs of your second-language parents as well as your students. In this way, you are sharing what you are covering in the classroom with your whole second language community.

Resources

Contents of Digital Resource CD

PDF Files

The full-color PDFs provided are each six pages long and contain all three levels of a reading passage. For example, *A Day in the Life of a Cowhand* PDF (pages 11–16) is the *cowhand.pdf* file.

Text Files

The Microsoft Word® documents include the text for all three levels of each reading passage. For example, *A Day in the Life of a Cowhand* text (pages 11–16) is the *cowhand.docx* file.

Text Title	Text File	PDF
A Day in the Life of a Cowhand	cowhand.docx	cowhand.pdf
Sweet: Inside a Bakery	bakery.docx	bakery.pdf
The Mystery of the Grand Bazaar	bazaar.docx	bazaar.pdf
How to Survive in the Jungle by the Person Who Knows	jungle.docx	jungle.pdf
Race to the Moon	race.docx	race.pdf
Our Vacation Budget	vacation.docx	vacation.pdf
Measuring Time	timing.docx	timing.pdf
Natural Measures	measures.docx	measures.pdf
My Lemonade Stand	lemonade.docx	lemonade.pdf
The World of Trade	trade.docx	trade.pdf
States of Matter	matter.docx	matter.pdf
Phases of the Moon	moon.docx	moon.pdf
Extreme Weather	weather.docx	weather.pdf
Photosynthesis	photo.docx	photo.pdf
Gravity	gravity.docx	gravity.pdf
Our Natural Resources	resources.docx	resources.pdf
The American Government	government.docx	government.pdf
America's Western Landmarks	landmark.docx	landmark.pdf
Doing Your Part	part.docx	part.pdf
America's National Capital	capital.docx	capital.pdf

Word Documents of Texts

- Change leveling further for individual students.
- Separate text and images for students who need additional help decoding the text.
- Resize the text for visually impaired students.

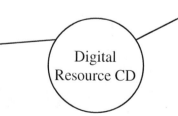

Full-Color PDFs of Texts

- Project texts for whole-class review.
- Post on your website and read texts online.
- Email texts to parents or students at home.